Dedicated to my

Ronald Robb Ritchie
and
Rodd Raoul Ritchie,

who are in the process of becoming
free at last
as they serve Him who is Life indeed!

ACKNOWLEDGMENTS

I am very grateful for the constant love, encouragement and support of my dear friends Eff and Patty Martin. They suggested that I put some of my teaching, which first appeared in "Discovery Papers," into a book—and wouldn't take "no" for an answer. I am also grateful for the privilege of walking alongside pastors, elders and God's people at Peninsula Bible Church in Palo Alto, California, since 1969. They are committed to Jesus Christ and growing together into a community that seeks to live their lives by the power of our risen Lord.

Special thanks to our cheerful editor, Susan Knepper, whose wonderful patience, humor and deadlines keep us all on schedule. I am also thankful to be surrounded by talented people like Sophia Beccue, a fine artist, and my long-time friends Don and Diana Corning, who introduced me to Eric Berendt, the cover-designer, and encouraged me with their creative ideas. They also provided the portrait for the cover. I want to express my eternal thankfulness to Anne Marie, my wife and best friend for almost four decades, who knows how long I have desired to be *free at last* and has stayed with me every step of the way.

With hearts full of joy, Anne Marie and I want to say thank you to Ray C. Stedman, who not only taught us the truth of becoming free in Christ, but continued to live in that freedom before us each day that we had the privilege of knowing him on this earth. Now he is truly *free at last*, in the presence of the Lord whom he loved so deeply.

TABLE OF CONTENTS

FOREWORD

I am extremely pleased to have a small part in the publication of *Free At Last!* Ron Ritchie is my best friend, a true friend in the deepest and most enduring sense of the word. He mentored my wife when she was an intern at Peninsula Bible Church before I met her. He trained me in my first serious opportunity for Christian leadership. He ministered at our wedding and dedicated each of our three children. He has laughed with us over a thousand happy meals in every part of the world. He wept with us when we lost a child and his wife healed our broken hearts when she assisted us in the adoption of our youngest daughter. He has encouraged me when I have been overwhelmed and rebuked me when I have forgotten that God is in control. For more than twenty years he has loved me and my family with the persistent love of Jesus Christ.

During those years he has taught me the revolutionary message of the new covenant from the pulpit and in his own life. *Free At Last!* is the outpouring of Ron's greatest passion. It is an exposition of the Lord's great plan that we should be free and joyful. We were never intended to bear the burdens of this life in our own strength. God has provided the power for us to face every challenge and to experience life with a richness beyond our wildest imaginings.

The power of the message of *Free At Last!* does not reside in Ron Ritchie; it flows from the heart of God. I feel, however, that Ron has done a superb job of clearly proclaiming and ill trating the way in which God designed life to be lived.

In my own life I have applied these principles somewhat inc sistently. However imperfectly I have put these truths into practice, at this point I cannot imagine trying to live based my own strength and abilities. I have learned that only thr daily dependence on Jesus Christ can we survive life's valle Perhaps more importantly, we can only realize our grande aspirations and fulfill our deepest longings through his p and direction. I hope that *Free At Last!* will help you to e ence the joy, excitement and peace of a life lived in reliar God rather than on yourself.

Eff W. Martin
January 18, 199

Chapter 1

Free-at Last!

TO LOVE GOD

If you hold to my teaching, you are really my disciples. Then you will know the truth, and the Truth will set you free.

- Jesus[1]

I would like to share part of my life to communicate the passion behind this book. I will start somewhere in the beginning—the beginning of my spiritual journey, that is, when my soul and spirit were dead, imprisoned by religious rituals and meaningless church activity.

In the Beginning…

My mother's parents came from Florence, Italy. In their day, everyone born in Italy was expected to observe the dominant religious traditions, including attending weekly worship services and all religious holiday celebrations. Leaving the "Old Country" in the early years of this century and immigrating to the United States of America filled the hearts of my "Papa" and my pregnant "Nana" with fear as well as hopeful dreams of a new start in their young lives. They arrived with their few belongings and passed through the famous Ellis Island in New York Harbor. Once settled in a row house in the "Little Italy" section of South Philadelphia, they found their culture, language and, of course, their religious heritage all intact. In this setting, "Papa" and "Nana" raised their four children, one of whom in time became my mother, Jessica.

As the children grew into adulthood, Jessica met a Scotsman named Theodore R. Ritchie, who came from a fairly stable background and had his own religious heritage, but of a different persuasion. They married and put their religious differences on the back burner until they had children. At that time my mother convinced my father that it would be best to raise the children according to her religion.

When I was about seven, something happened to my mother's religion. She had taken a pair of shoes to a Polish shoemaker to have the soles repaired. The shoemaker told her that she needed her *soul* fixed as well. He encouraged my mother to ask Jesus Christ to become her Lord, receive his forgiveness for her sins and replace her religious activities with a personal relationship with Jesus. An event like that can change your religious heritage in a hurry. Suddenly, without warning (or so it seemed to a young boy), she was telling her husband, children, parents and friends that she had "become a Christian." (I had thought we were Christians all along!) The fact that a chain smoker like her quit smoking proved to me that a very real change had occurred.

Shortly after that time, we moved to a small river town north of Philadelphia, called Bristol. Our family, except for my father, became involved in a whole new realm of religious activities. We attended a local church every Sunday. I remember that we would sing for a long time and then a pastor would teach from the Bible. Now that was really a whole new approach to our religious experience. During the three years we attended that church, I remember singing "Onward Christian Soldiers" countless times. We all expected Jesus to come back to earth at any moment.

In the midst of this joyful new experience, everything changed again. When I was twelve, I came home from school one October afternoon to find my mother and our new baby sister crying. I learned from my eleven-year-old sister that our father had walked out on the family, leaving us desolate. When our pastor heard this news, he arranged to have all three of us children placed in an orphanage until my mother could figure out what to do. That process took eight years!

My oldest sister and I were sent to a "Christian" orphanage located on a 365-acre farm in the northern suburbs of Philadelphia. (Our baby sister was placed in an orphanage in Lancaster, some 50 miles away.) Our "home" was run by first-generation German-Americans who believed in God and hard work. They lived by an extremely strict set of cultural taboos, which prohibited smoking, drinking, going to movies, and so forth. During those years, I was unknowingly caught up in "Christian legalism." I tried in my own strength to keep the Law of God as well as all those cultural taboos (which kept changing once television arrived on the scene). In that "Christian" atmosphere I began to hate anything that had to do with religion, including the people involved.

The Middle

In my senior year of high school, I was drafted to fight in the Korean War. I was finally on my own, going through Air Force Basic Training in upstate New York and being forced to attend Chapel services eight Sundays in a row. I was then shipped to Waco, Texas, where I also attended night school at Baylor University. There I met a group of southern folks who spoke a lot of religion with an accent. On Sundays they all went to church because at that time Baylor was a "religious" university. In order to be with my new friends, I attended a local church which was led by a dynamic pastor—who later ran off with his choir director. This seemed normal to me at the time, but my religious friends were shocked.

That winter, when I received word that my father lay dying in a Pennsylvania hospital, the Air Force gave me emergency leave. I had only seen him a few times over the previous eight years, which had given me the chance to cultivate a very bitter heart. I was not prepared for what I saw when I walked into that hospital room and looked down on the skeleton of his former self on the verge of death. In spite of my hard feelings, I found a local pastor I had known in my high school days and brought him to my father. (I must have gotten the idea from a movie.) I stood by the door and listened as this pastor spoke to my father, who lay under an oxygen tent.

"Mr. Ritchie, Jesus loves you and wants you to acknowledge your need of him as your savior. If you ask him, he will forgive all your sins, come into your life and give you the gift of eternal life. Now I know that you cannot speak, but if you want to invite Jesus to come into your life, just squeeze my hand."

A few seconds passed in silence. Then, with eyes of disbelief, I saw my dying father squeeze the pastor's hand, signifying that finally, after all those years, he had bowed his proud heart and knee to God. The pastor was thrilled. He prayed and thanked God for his love for my father and the gift of eternal life.

I left in anger. It was not fair; this was just too simple. Certainly my father had to pay for all the sorrow, pain and grief he had caused my mother and her three children. I went out on a date that evening with an old girl friend. The next day I returned to the hospital only to find my father's room completely empty. A nurse asked if she could help me, and I said I was looking for Mr. Ritchie. She said, "Oh! He died last night. Are you a relative?" "No! Just his son," I replied, and walked out. After the funeral, I returned to Texas, hard-hearted and dry-eyed.

Back in Waco, I rejoined my new set of "religious" friends. I had had my fill of "religion," but these students, especially a senior named Jo Ann, were quietly disarming me with their genuine faith in God. She was probably the closest I had ever come to Jesus, Mary and Joseph all wrapped up in one. In the middle of the spring quarter, I received my military orders to go to North Africa, because the war in Korea had ended. Jo Ann and her friends all gathered to say good-bye to me and told me they would pray for me. I hid the tears with a tough, "Hey, we'll get together again," and caught a train to Philadelphia for a few weeks with my mother, sisters and grandparents.

I then continued up to New York to board the ship along with several hundred other GI's. A light rain began to fall as many of us leaned on the railing of the ship looking down on the families who were waving good-bye to their sons. A military band on the dock played several patriotic songs. As the ship pulled away from the dock, the band played "Oh My Papa," a very familiar tune in the early 1950s, sung by Eddie Fisher. That song was written by a son who, having just lost his father in death, remembers how wonderful he had been in life. As the tugboats pushed the ship away from the dock, warm tears flooded my eyes, but were hidden by the gentle rain falling on my face. To this day, whenever I hear that song, my heart fills with tears as my mind races back to that moment.

It took nine days to sail to Casablanca, Morocco. As soon as we arrived, many of us were placed on a train and sent north to the capital city of Rabat, which was to become my home for the next three and a half years. There I began a new season of "wine, women, and song." I became a disc jockey at our local radio station. Through this job, I met all kinds of people and I soon discovered that I could smoke, drink, dance, chew, and do anything I wanted. I had plenty of distractions to fill my free time: lovely French girls, beautiful sandy beaches, delicious French and Moroccan food, dances at the club, and flights to Tangiers, Madrid, Paris, Cairo—all this with no weekly religious interruption. Inside, however, I was having a moral struggle with this lifestyle.

For the first time after a year in the service, I was settled into "normal" living. I decided that it was time to continue my voice training, which I had neglected since high school. I soon discovered that the wife of one of my officers was a talented music director and led the choir in the only Protestant church in town.

Well, it was time to get into "religion" again, especially if it could meet my needs. I joined the choir and was asked to sing solos on several occasions, especially religious holidays.

My participation in the choir opened up an opportunity to join the local chaplain and some two dozen other GI's on a religious retreat to Israel. One cold October morning, I took a walk down a narrow alley in Jerusalem. I soon came to a door with a sign that read "The Garden Tomb." I knocked and the door slowly began to open. On the other side stood a pleasant Palestinian man who invited me inside. I asked him about the garden, and he told me that the Protestant Christians thought this was the place where Jesus was buried after he died on the cross. He invited me to look around the beautiful garden where Jesus had allegedly risen from the dead.

I soon found myself alone, except for the gardener. I approached the "cave," looked inside, and finally decided to stoop down and walk in. This cave had been chiseled out of the side of a large rock wall and was big enough to hold one body on the stone floor and several mourners. I sat in the mourners section for a long time, and began to think about Jesus, the cross and the resurrection. Then a strange thing happened. I found myself praying to a God I really did not know and had no plans to know: "If there is really a God, I want the God of Jo Ann to come into my heart and change my messed-up life."

Nothing happened. That is, there was no bright light, no angelic choir, no brass band—just a quiet sense of rest and peace. I stood up and noticed a sign on the inside wall that read, "He is not here for he has risen." I stooped once again to exit, said good-bye to my Palestinian host, and walked back out into the Jerusalem morning. Later that week, the chaplain arranged a religious service on the grounds of the Garden of Gethsemane. He asked me to sing an old hymn I had sung several times as a youth, "I Come to the Garden Alone." This time, I sang it with new meaning.

I returned to Rabat and soon fell back into my old habits of wine, women, and Thursday night choir practice with the colonel's wife. But some drastic changes were beginning to occur. One Saturday night, I got drunk at the NCO club and returned to my room very sick and tired at around 2:00 AM. I fell into bed fully clothed. Suddenly, or so it seemed, a loud knock on my door caused me to bolt up in bewilderment. I struggled to open the door, and despite the haze of my hangover, recognized my two best friends, Ted and John. They told me it was 8:00 AM and they were on their way to breakfast. They also invited me to their room that night for a Bible study they were going to start. I told them I would be there at 1800 hours and fell back into bed exhausted. My last thoughts were, "A Bible study led by my two drinking buddies—too much!"

For the next two years, we studied the Gospel of John and snacked on peanut butter and jelly sandwiches while trying to grasp what it meant. That little study group grew so big that we moved to our military base a few miles outside of town where we met in a wooden hut. In time, some 200 GI's and their girlfriends or wives joined us in music, prayer, teaching from the Bible and an improvement—tuna sandwiches.

During this season, I met a wonderful French girl named Anne Marie. We worked together, but were dating other people. As we discussed "religion" around a pot-bellied stove in our office, we discovered we were falling in love with each other. She had come from the same religious background as I, so we had both had a good dose of rituals. Anne Marie had always loved Jesus, but did not understand the need to invite him into her heart in order to establish a personal relationship with him as her Lord and Savior. Since I had invited Jesus into my heart in Jerusalem, I was hoping she would do the same so that we would have a common spiritual foundation. I had heard somewhere that this was a good thing if you were thinking of marriage. I was! And she did! We were married in the one and only local Protestant church, where I was a member of the choir.

After a year of marriage, my four-year-three-month-sixteen-day-and-nine-hour obligation to the Air Force was over. Based on our great experience with our "church" on the base, Anne Marie and I came to the conclusion that we should go into some kind of work that would help others. At the time we were considering the field of psychology. We made plans to go to college in the States on the GI Bill. We boarded the *SS Rose* out of Casablanca, and nine days later passed by the Statue of Liberty and disembarked in New York City.

We headed for Pennsylvania to stay at my mother's home for a few months until we could get our feet on the ground culturally and choose a college to attend. Mother belonged to a very conservative local church which supported a Bible School with the same convictions. Anne Marie and I decided to begin our education at this small school until we had a better picture of the college scene. In our classes in a small farm house on the outskirts of town, we were taught that being a Christian meant not wearing lipstick or listening to jazz. I had dozens of great jazz records that I had brought home from Morocco. The teachers eventually convinced us to burn them.

What a shock to our spiritual system! After two years we moved on to another Bible college and discovered that they, as well as many of the churches we attended, also had a long list of rules which served as a barometer of your spiritual life. In both schools we found that Christianity was a lifestyle in which you did *not* do certain things, such as play cards, go to the movies, gamble, or smoke, to mention but a few. Over the years I have often looked back at these "religious experiences" and thought how odd it was that we never received a "To Do" list with imperatives such as, "Love one another, pray for one another, encourage one another, speak in love to one another, forgive one another!"

Following those two religious experiences, a pastor friend encouraged me to go to seminary. Many of the instructors there had come from the above two schools, so the incoming class naturally received a list of rules that still included, "no smoking, no movies, no…." For my own sanity, I signed the list and then added a postscript.: "I disagree with all of the above statements, but I will abide by the above in order to get my degree." Instinctively, I felt this was the wrong approach. Later, I would learn why. I then began my third major religious experience, kicking and screaming all the way.

The End…of Legalism or, Free at Last

In my second year of seminary, one of my professors invited me and thirteen other men to a weekend retreat to meet his best friend, Ray Stedman, "from California." (We were intrigued by the fact that he was from such an "exotic" place!) Ray taught us from the first six chapters of Second Corinthians. I listened intently as he explained certain spiritual principles, such as the meaning of Jesus' statement, "Without me you can do nothing;" and the implications of the Apostle Paul's words, "We learned to no longer trust in ourselves but in God who raises the dead." When he spoke of the "ministry of the Spirit," and no longer living for ourselves but for him who died and rose again on our behalf, my heart was full of joy and fear at the same time.

It seemed that all of my life had been controlled by one form of religion or another: "Do this! Don't do that!" I was so threatened by Ray's teaching that I found myself arguing with him over many of his statements. If he was right, my whole religious system was heading down the tube. With a spirit of grace, he listened to me and then slowly answered each of my questions. Every answer confirmed what I suspected true Christianity should be, but had rarely witnessed. By the end of the weekend, I found myself hugging him with tears running down my cheeks. I was *free to love God*, and to love others in the power of the resurrected Jesus, who lived in me and wanted to express himself through me. As I drove home, I was amazed how free I felt—free not to live my life for myself, but *free at last* to be like Jesus and live my new life in him to his delight and my joy.

I met Ray again when I moved to the San Francisco Bay Area to take a job. He eventually asked me if I would consider working with him and the other free men and women on the staff of Peninsula Bible Church in Palo Alto. I accepted in the summer of 1969 and since then, have been earnestly learning how to enjoy living out what the "man from California" called "authentic Christianity." He said he himself learned this spiritual truth from the Word of God and from several important men in his generation who demonstrated it for him, such as Dr. Harry Ironside and Dr. J. Vernon McGee.

Each generation needs to take this wonderful truth of being free to live like Jesus and pass it on to the next generation. The following is my humble attempt to "pass it on" to the next generation. I hope that my new life, which is still in the process of becoming more and more like Jesus, will speak louder than my written words.

Chapter 2

Free at Last!

TO BE AT PEACE

"The Lord blesses his people with Peace."
- David[1]

In every generation God raises up individuals who are able to help us remember the spiritual realities of our relationship with Jesus Christ. They help us understand our calling to trust him with our daily lives, rather than submit to the stress of trying to meet the demands of various religious or spiritual systems. One of those godly men today is Charles Colson, founder of Prison Fellowship Ministries, who served time in jail himself for breaking the law when he was an aide to President Nixon. While in prison he had a personal encounter with Jesus Christ and received a "Life Sentence" in which God called him to minister to prisoners around the world.

Living In a Stressful "Post–Christian" World

In his book, *The Body: Being Light in Darkness*, Colson explains the current definition of truth in Western society and shows how it directly opposes the truth found in the teachings of Jesus Christ. He reminds his readers that current Western thinking is built on the foundation of relativism, the belief that there are no absolutes in truth and morals (except the absolute that there can be no absolutes). In other words, truth is determined by a majority vote. Colson writes, "Although the West is still called a

'Christian culture' by some, it is not. It is distinctly post-Christian, dominated by a relativistic world-view."[2]

This "post-Christian world" with its changing philosophies causes many of us to stumble, and we can suffer some very damaging consequences as we try to cope with this negative pressure. This stress can take a toll not only on our own lives, but in time on our family, business and social relationships. Some among us are wise enough to try to find a way to address this problem with the help of professional and spiritual counselors and groups. Others unfortunately permit stress not only to enter their lives, but to control them to the point where their only hope of relief is drinking, drugs, or the ultimate escape—suicide.

Self Help and New Age Groups

Among the many resources available to help us battle the stress factor are two old philosophies offering relief under new names. I'm referring to the "Self Help" and "New Age" movements. Most bookstores now stock scores of new books and magazines on these two subjects. If you don't like to read, these teachings are also readily available on slickly packaged video or audio cassettes. Bookstores and cafés are often plastered with dozens of fliers about new spiritual teachers and new seminars offering consumers more hope for peace of mind, body and spirit. The ultimate aim of the self-help movement, as the titles proclaim, is ego massage. I recently saw an advertisement for the ultimate ego trip, "How To Be A Winner." This package proclaimed that you could be a winner by developing your capacity for self-achievement, self-motivation, self-control and self-esteem. *Self* is the name of the game. This has been the philosophy of every generation since man first walked on the face of the earth. It may appear under different names and guises, but it is still the philosophy that contends that you are the master of your fate; take control of your life and be a winner.

The "New Age" movement, on the other hand, promises to

deliver you from stress by addressing your spiritual nature or soul. New Age advocates have become disenchanted with secular ways of thinking. They claim to have "new" perspectives, such as, "All is one," and "All is God." God is referred to as "She," "It," or as in *Star Wars*, "The Force." One New Age writer claims, "We are all gods whether we realize it or not. We need to awaken the god who sleeps at the root of our humanity." This philosophy, of course, is but another encapsulation of Hinduism, Buddhism, and the ideas of self-appointed Eastern mystics. I have a friend who was born in India, later moved to the United States, and in time established a personal relationship with Jesus Christ. Her father, however, is still a well-known spiritual teacher within Hinduism. I once asked my friend why her father was so attracted to that form of religion. I will never forget her answer: "Oh Ron, it's so simple. We would all rather *be* a god than serve one!"

Unfortunately, some followers of Jesus Christ are being tempted to find relief from stress in the ways these movements advocate. Christians should know, however, that it was not God's intent for people to respond to stress by proclaiming themselves to be winners or gods.

Peace of Mind in the Midst of Stress

The question we need to ask in these stressful times is, "Does God have a better arrangement for living, regardless of the current stressful circumstances of our society?" I submit to you that the answer is, yes! A thousand times yes! And I would like you to consider that since the dawn of mankind, the only living, true and wise God, who has clearly revealed himself in his Son Jesus Christ, has offered a better arrangement for living—including coping with stress. God designed us to live this life in complete dependence on him for the strength to cope with our present realities. At times God allows stress to come into our lives to help us learn that we are not able to live life depending on our own personality, power, or position.

Exhibit A

The authors of the Bible give us several examples of how Jesus was able to hold up under tremendous stress during his ministry on earth. As you read the writings of his disciples Matthew, Mark, Luke and John, you soon discover that Jesus taught them and all who would follow him that the secret of holding up under stress came from his vital relationship with his Heavenly Father. He said in essence, "I don't say anything, do anything, or go anywhere without first checking in with my Heavenly Father. For my will is to do the will of my Father who is in heaven."[3]

One of the most stressful times in Jesus' life occurred when he was struggling with his Heavenly Father about going to the cross to die for the sins of mankind. He went to the Garden of Gethsemane with his disciples to pray about the whole situation, "and being in anguish, he prayed more earnestly; and his sweat was like drops of blood falling to the ground. When he rose from prayer and went back to his disciples, he found them asleep, exhausted from sorrow. 'Why are you sleeping?' he asked them. 'Get up and pray so that you will not fall into temptation.'"[4] A short while later, Jesus' disciple Judas betrayed him. When the authorities arrested Jesus, his other friends also abandoned him. He endured a trial, beatings, and ridicule. Jesus was then forced to carry his own cross to the hill of Calvary outside the gates of Jerusalem, where he willingly suffered an undeserved, painful death—for our sins, not his.

How did Jesus cope with that overwhelming stress? We see the key in his prayer in the garden just before his arrest. Jesus models for us his lifestyle of full dependence upon the presence and power of his Heavenly Father. He prayed not only for himself, but also for his disciples then and in every age to come.

I am coming to you now, but I say these things
while I am still in the world, so that they may
have the full measure of my joy within them.

I have given them your word and the world has hated them, for they are not of the world any more than I am of the world. My prayer is not that you take them out of the world, but that you protect them from the evil one....My prayer is not for them alone, I pray also for those who will believe in me through their message, that all of them may be one.[5]

One of Jesus' disciples named Peter, who at the crucial moment gave in to the pressure and denied his Lord, later revealed the secret of Jesus' inner strength. In 62 AD he wrote a letter to a group of persecuted Christians in Turkey:

If you suffer for doing good and you endure it, this is commendable before God. To this you were called, because Christ suffered for you, leaving you an example, that you should follow in his steps. He committed no sin, and no deceit was found in his mouth. When they hurled their insults at him he did not retaliate; when he suffered, he made no threats. Instead, he *entrusted himself* to him [his Heavenly Father] who judges justly.[6]

Exhibit B

The apostle Paul also experienced great temptation to succumb to stress while he was trying to bring the good news of Jesus Christ to the various people groups within the Roman Empire. As we look at his second letter to the church in Corinth, we learn how Paul was able to maintain an "inner peace" although daily faced with stress from those who hated him, plans that went awry, and false prophets who sought to discredit him. We will learn from Paul the secrets of our own humanity, and how God designed us to live and deal with stress. Stress itself is not the issue; what's important is how we handle it. We have a choice:

allow stress to control us, or give it over to Jesus and let him give us the strength to resist its crushing force. In a real sense, we live in the world system, but by God's grace and power, we also can be set free from its compelling influences, anxieties and pressure.

Setting the Stage

Before we delve into Paul's second letter to the Church in Corinth, we need to understand the apostle's personal history as well as the makeup of the Corinthian Church. Paul's formal name was Saul. He was born to a Jewish family who lived in the coastal city of Tarsus, located in the southern part of present-day Turkey. He became a Jewish teacher, a leader in the religious community, and in time joined in persecuting the followers of Jesus. On one of his journeys to arrest some of those Christians, he encountered the resurrected Jesus on the road to Damascus, Syria. It was here that Paul gave his life to the Lord, who in turn empowered him with his Holy Spirit. Jesus set Paul free to tell the Jewish people (and later the Gentiles) that he was the Messiah who greatly loved them. Paul's task was to explain to all who would listen that Jesus wanted to give them the gift of salvation. All they had to do was place their faith in him as their one and only Savior—the Savior who would not only forgive their sins, but deliver them from the power of sin and fear of death. Paul had already been sharing the good news of Jesus Christ with hundreds of Jews and Gentiles by the time he wrote this letter to the Christians in Corinth.

Several years after he met the risen Jesus on the Road to Damascus, Paul became one of the pastors of a church in Antioch, located in modern-day Lebanon. This church sent him and his friend Barnabas on what has come to be known as "the first missionary journey" into Turkey. They returned to Antioch and reported that many people had responded to the good news of Jesus Christ and had become "Christ followers." The church of Antioch then sent Paul and Silas on "the second missionary journey," which took them back to visit the churches of Turkey:

Derbe, Iconium, Antioch and Lystra (where they met a young man named Timothy and asked him to join them).

While the men were visiting the western port city of Troas, Paul received a vision from God in which he saw a man calling him to come over into the Greek district of Macedonia. So in 52 AD he, Timothy and Silas headed west, were joined by a Gentile doctor named Luke, and over the next several months established churches in the Greek cities of Philippi, Thessalonica and Berea. Then Paul left Timothy and Silas in Berea, traveled south to Athens, and finally ended up in the port city of Corinth, where he met a Jewish couple named Aquila and Priscilla, and worked with them at the trade of tent making. On the Sabbath, these three tentmakers would go to the synagogue to preach to the Jews and God-fearing Greeks that salvation could now be found in a spiritual relationship with their resurrected Messiah, Jesus. When Silas and Timothy arrived in Corinth from Macedonia, Paul decided to devote himself full-time to teaching the word of God and testifying to the Jews that Jesus was their Messiah. Many of the Jews resisted the message and blasphemed; so he declared to them, "Your blood be upon your own heads! I am clear of my responsibility. From now on, I will go to the Gentiles" (the non-Jewish population of Romans, Greeks and other people groups). He stayed with his fellow workers for the next eighteen months and shared the gospel with the non-Jewish people of the city. Soon a church was established.[7]

Then Paul and his team traveled on to Ephesus, Turkey, and on to Jerusalem. Some five years later (about 57 AD), conflict broke out between the apostle and the Corinthian church over how the spiritual leaders should treat followers of Jesus who were living a lifestyle that violated his teachings, especially in the area of sexual immorality. He also received the bad news that some false apostles had infiltrated the church,[8] confusing the believers and launching an attack on his ministry, personality, and apostolic authority. These events caused him much grief and anguish of spirit. He wrote four letters to the Corinthian church to seek reconciliation. His first letter is referred to today as the "lost letter." In it he dealt with the issue of whether the church should permit fellowship with believers who were involved in sexual immorality.[9] Then he wrote a second letter, which survived as First Corinthians. This was a pastoral letter, in which he encouraged the Corinthians to avoid competition amongst themselves and to flee sexual immorality.

Paul made a quick visit to Corinth, and what he found there was devastating. Upon his return to Ephesus he wrote a "painful letter," which is also lost to us. In this letter, hand-carried by a disciple named Titus, he asked the Corinthians to deal with sexual immorality within the church, and he again sought reconciliation with the Corinthians. Then he stayed in the western port city of Troas hoping for Titus to return quickly and bring some good news about their receptivity to his painful letter. Once Titus arrived, Paul learned that his spiritual children in Corinth had accepted his loving rebuke and were reconciled to him. At that time he wrote a "thankful letter" to them. In this fourth letter, Second Corinthians, Paul describes how he felt as he waited in Troas for Titus to return with their response to his painful letter.

Freedom in the Presence of the Lord

In his account of the "season of stress" which he underwent as he awaited word from Corinth, the apostle Paul reveals to us some of the mystery of his relationship with Jesus, together with some of the spiritual principles that enabled him to cope with reality in a difficult, stressful world. His words will enable us to address the questions: How can we find freedom to enjoy peace of mind in the midst of a society in which stress is causing men and women all around us to crumble physically, emotionally and spiritually? How can we find spiritual freedom when we are pressured on every side to submit to the changing values arising from current world philosophies?

> Now when I went to Troas to preach the gospel
> of Christ and found that the Lord had opened a
> door for me, I still had no peace of mind, because
> I did not find my brother Titus there. So I said
> good-by to them and went on to Macedonia.[10]

Troas, where Paul sat awaiting Titus, was a Roman colony, named Alexandria Troas in honor of Alexander the Great. By 57 AD the city was a flourishing little Rome, basking in many political privileges granted by Caesar. This was where, some five years earlier, Paul had had a vision of a Macedonian begging him to come to Macedonia and help.[11] He was quite familiar with this city, located some 150 miles north of Ephesus, and knew a group of Christians there. He went to Troas with a two-fold agenda— to wait for Titus, and to preach the gospel.

Paul was delighted to preach the good news of Jesus Christ to anyone who would listen because that message of hope had so changed his life. The change began in his heart and transformed his whole lifestyle. Anger, hatred, pride and murder, gave way to a life which increasingly resembled Jesus' genuine love for God and people from every walk of life, every culture, race and religion. Once he settled in Corinth, he took the opportunity to summarize the message in a letter to the Christians in Rome:

> If you confess with your mouth, 'Jesus is Lord,'
> and believe in your heart that God raised him
> from the dead, you will be saved. For it is with
> your heart that you believe and are justified, and
> it is with your mouth that you confess and are
> saved. As the Scripture says, 'Anyone who trusts
> in him will never be put to shame.' For there is
> no difference between Jew and Gentile—the
> same Lord is Lord of all and richly blesses all
> who call on him, for 'Everyone who calls on the
> name of the Lord will be saved.'"[12]

What a great message to hear! If we respond to this message of love, we are set free from having to appear before God for our sin of rejecting his Son as our Savior. We are also set free from the power of Satan, the fear of death, and eternal separation from our Creator. The moment we place our faith in him as our Lord, we receive the gift of eternal life, as well as the gift of the person and power of the Holy Spirit to enable us to cope with life on this earth. Talk about freedom and peace of mind!

Not only was Paul willing and ready to share the good news about Jesus, he was also keenly aware of the presence of the resurrected Lord going before him, opening some doors of opportunity and closing others. As he stood in the marketplace in Troas, his heart must have been beating with joy and fear as he anticipated the Lord working through him. He was probably encouraged by his friends to make good use of this open door to proclaim the good news of Christ. But, amazingly, despite the open door, despite the presence of the resurrected Lord and the assurance of his spiritual family, Paul says, "I still had no peace of mind, because I did not find my brother Titus there."

With those words, "I still had no peace of mind," we get a glimpse of Paul's human weakness. He was a man filled with the Holy Spirit, convinced that the Lord was at work through him, and yet he found no rest in his spirit. He was becoming anxious about the return of Titus with word of the Corinthians' response to his "painful letter." Until Titus arrived, he would have no peace of mind, no rest in his spirit. Where was the wisdom in starting a new work in Troas if his spiritual family in Corinth was still struggling over whether he was a genuine apostle of Christ? During that time of restlessness he probably wondered if the Corinthians were still angry with him or if they had read the letter and repented. Should he return to Corinth again and try to resolve that situation before beginning a new ministry? Stress was running high for Paul as he struggled between staying where the door was wide open for ministry, or leaving town to go look for Titus in Greece, in hopes that he would have good news from the Corinthians.

Enough time had passed for Titus to have completed his trip to Corinth and then back to Troas. As a result of his anxiety, Paul decided to leave for Macedonia, Greece, perhaps hoping to find Titus at the church in Philippi. Later in this letter he writes, "For when we came into Macedonia, this body of ours had no rest, but we were harassed at every turn—conflicts on the outside, fears within."[13] So Paul suffered a great deal of stress in Troas as well as on his journey westward to the church in Philippi. His struggle seemed to be between what he thought was good and what was best in the sight of God.

I have been amazed over the years how the Lord will allow us to face more open doors of opportunity than we could ever possibly enter. We have our family responsibilities, and many open doors in our immediate neighborhood, through community events, sports programs or camp experiences. Of course, there are also political committees, social committees, religious committees, as well as great opportunities for social service offered at our place of employment. Then if we go to our local churches, we discover more open doors of ministry within the children's programs, high school programs, college programs, singles programs, adult programs—all needing teachers, workers, drivers and money. Just about the time we think we are comfortably committed, the missions committee informs us of all the open doors of ministry around the world. More stress begins to build as we realize we have already said yes to too many other "good" things!

What is a person to do? How do we distinguish the good from the best amidst all these calls? How can we maintain peace of mind in the midst of our stressful world?

We need to be conscious of the presence of the Lord and his willingness to work with us as we make certain choices. But we must also be aware that our walk of faith is not computer-programmed to guarantee that if we follow all the steps page by page, we will experience immediate success. Paul illustrated in his life that he was keenly aware of the presence of the Lord. But he also was a man in the process of becoming mature in his relationship with Jesus. There is no such thing as instant spiritual maturity. The key to maintaining peace of mind is learning to trust that God is at work. Even when we choose to walk away from open doors of opportunity, God can use our lives to bring great blessings to us and to others, as we will see.

Paul goes on to give us more insight into his relationship with the Lord. That relationship enabled him to look at his stressful situation and still be conscious of the presence of God, as well as the power of God. Only God's strength could overcome Paul's failure and weakness and produce a life of triumph in the midst of stress.

Freedom and the Power of God

> But thanks be to God, who always leads us in triumphal procession in Christ and through us spreads everywhere the fragrance of the knowledge of him. For we are to God the aroma of Christ among those who are being saved and those who are perishing. To the one we are the smell of death; to the other, the fragrance of life. And who is equal to such a task? Unlike so many, we do not peddle the word of God for profit. On the contrary, in Christ we speak before God with sincerity, like men sent from God.[14]

This passage is about making choices. As we go through it, it is important to keep in mind the role the Holy Spirit plays in the choices we make. Let me explain. Do you remember when I told you that I went to that empty tomb in Jerusalem and sat down on the cold stone floor and began to speak to "God?" Well, at that moment I was a man with no spiritual life. I had lived out my life as if I were God, so I only reported to myself as the final authority. The words written by one of Jesus's disciples named John around 90 AD addressed my life at that point: "Do not love the world [system] or anything in the world. If anyone loves the world, the love of the Father is not in him. For everything in the world—the cravings of sinful man, the lust of his eyes and the boasting of what he has and does—comes not from the Father but from the world. The world and its desires pass away, but the man who does the will of God lives forever."[15]

After I gave my life to God, I discovered that my heart was filled with a love for him. I wanted to choose to live for him day by day. This was now possible because the moment I placed my faith in Jesus, he gave me eternal life and his Holy Spirit. For the first time in my life, I discovered that God had given me the power to make lifestyle choices to be like him—willing to serve others unselfishly, with an attitude of love and gentleness.

The late Ray Stedman, pastor for some four decades at Peninsula Bible Church in Palo Alto, California, often reminded his friends in the Christian community: "We have never been given the power to do, only the power to choose. What we choose determines what we do. If we choose as Christians to follow our own fleshly desires, the flesh takes over and produces death. If we choose to follow the leading of the Holy Spirit, he takes over our lives and produces life." The indwelling Holy Spirit, then, is the one who gives us the power to reject our old fleshly desires and to choose to make godly decisions. Once we make a decision to be like Jesus, he provides the necessary power to carry out our godly desires.

We should be greatly encouraged by Paul. As he sought to make Christlike choices in his corrupt world, so we should be seeking to make Christlike choices in our corrupt, post-Christian society, relying on the Holy Spirit to develop within us a godly lifestyle. Those who are presently living in a dark and hopeless world will then see the life and light of Jesus within us. They may even be drawn by his love and mercy to ask us about the source of our joy, freedom and peace when facing the same circumstances.

Thankful Regardless

One important choice that Paul made was to have a grateful heart. "But thanks be to God...." Paul challenges the current world-view of naturalism, which denies the existence of the supernatural, by breaking out in thanksgiving to the one and only living God who is above and beyond his creation. What has happened to Paul to make him utter this sudden cry of thankfulness? It's obvious he is not thankful for having to write his painful letter to the Corinthians, not finding Titus in Troas, or learning that the church in Corinth was being subverted by false apostles. Nor is he thankful for his conflict with the church there, for the lost opportunity to preach the good news about Jesus at Troas, or for the stress he experienced on his journey to Macedonia. We discover the reason for his thankfulness later in this letter:

> For even when we came into Macedonia this body of ours had no rest, but we were harassed at every turn—conflicts on the outside, fears within. But God, who comforts the downcast, comforted us by the coming of Titus, and not only by his coming but also by the comfort you had given him. He told us about your longing for me, your deep sorrow, your ardent concern for me, so that my joy was greater than ever.[16]

Paul was thankful that God was able to work above and beyond his stressful circumstances, particularly when all he could do was pray. Paul couldn't change the hearts of the Corinthians. Titus reported to him that the Corinthians had accepted the painful letter. They had changed their attitude toward him, and they were dealing with the issue of sexual immorality in the church. Paul had no peace of mind in Troas while he waited for Titus. He was harassed at every turn on his way to Macedonia, but God was already at work changing the hearts of the Corinthians. No wonder he is able to say, "Thanks be to God!" God works in a much greater way than we can ever ask or think.

The foundational principle of Paul's life was thankfulness. He encouraged the Thessalonian church, "...in everything give thanks; for this is God's will for you in Christ Jesus."[17] True thankfulness is a rare commodity in these days of stress. As followers of Jesus, we are instructed to choose to ask him to fill our hearts with gratefulness. We realize that he is above and beyond his creation and thus only he is free to work out all our present circumstances to his honor and glory and our personal joy. When we choose to allow God to produce a "thankful heart" within us regardless of our immediate circumstances, many people in our community, workplace, or extended family will be curious enough to ask about the source of our "inner strength," giving us the opportunity to speak about our relationship with Jesus and how he is changing our lives from the inside out.

Another dramatic instance of this truth in Paul's life occurred later when he was a prisoner being taken by ship from Turkey to Rome to appear before Caesar. A severe storm on the Adriatic Sea raged for two weeks and it appeared that all 276 sailors, Roman soldiers, and other prisoners would perish. In the midst of the storm, an angel of the Lord assured Paul that no one would die, but told him that the ship would be destroyed. Paul passed this message on to the men, and reminded them of it again on the last day as they were waiting for daylight so they could run the ship aground. He admonished them to eat, and "after he said this, he took some bread and *gave thanks to God in front of them all.* Then he broke it and began to eat. They were all encouraged and ate some food themselves."[18]

Triumph in Christ

Paul expresses his thankfulness to God, "who always leads us in triumphal procession in Christ." In these words, he illustrates the truth that no matter what the circumstances, even those that look like utter defeat, Jesus' disciples are always victorious in their walk with him. We can't lose! Paul compares the Christian's victory with the spectacle of the triumphal processions for

Roman generals in the first century AD. To be honored in this way, a general must have: served as the supreme commander in the battlefield, defeated and pacified the enemy, brought his troops home safely, gained new territory, and won a victory over a foreign power. These processions were awe-inspiring. The whole populace of Rome flocked to see the parade, which was led by standard-bearers carrying the flags of the various military units, closely followed by a statue of Jupiter, the supreme god of Rome. Then came carts containing the spoils of war, paintings and models of the conquered territory, musicians playing pipes, and white bulls which were to be sacrificed to the gods. Prisoners in chains marched to their death, followed by horn-blowers, priests swinging pots of incense, and captured kings and chieftains riding in carts. The victorious general drove a golden chariot drawn by four white horses while a slave held the wreath of Jupiter over his head. The general's family and the victorious army in full uniform marched in the procession, and the Roman senators and magistrates brought up the rear.[19]

The apostle uses the image of a Roman triumphal procession to illustrate the glory of the Christian's everyday experience in Christ. The victorious generals of Rome might get one or perhaps two triumphal parades in their lifetime, yet disciples of Jesus experience this victory every day. He wins spiritual battles over spiritual forces, the influences of our old nature and the world system. When things seem to be falling apart, Christians can proclaim victory no matter what the circumstances—at home, at work and play, in line at the unemployment office, at the side of an abandoned family, or at the grave of a friend or loved one. We are in Christ; therefore, all through our lives we are part of his continuing triumphal procession. As a friend in the midst of losing his job and home recently told me, "Even when it looks like nothing is happening, I know something good is happening beyond time and space because God is in charge."

The Fragrance of Life

Further, Paul says, "...through us [God] spreads everywhere the fragrance of the knowledge of him." Here the apostle is thinking of how the pagan priests from the Roman temples would carry incense pots to greet the returning victorious army. The fragrance of the incense would float over the whole triumphal procession. Paul compares Christians to incense pots: we carry within us the aroma of the life of Jesus so that those who come in contact with us experience the fragrance of his love for them. Christians will take that aroma of Christ into all kinds of situations. The fragrance will not disappear nor will it be restricted. It will linger long after we have left any group, individual, or situation.

For example, my wife and I had developed a friendly relationship with one of our neighbors over a period of several years. One day he called and for the first time wanted to talk to me about spiritual things. Over lunch he asked me about our lives, especially our spiritual lives, which he had observed in several different settings. I had the opportunity to tell him about how my wife and I encountered Jesus Christ as a young couple while living in Africa. I explained to him how we returned to the States intent on serving Jesus rather than ourselves. God had provided his Spirit to continue maturing in our spiritual lives, which in turn filled our hearts with a love for him and his children.

After lunch, my neighbor said he had to go for a walk on the beach. I went home thinking that I had just wasted my time because he did not seem very interested in Jesus after all. Three days later, I opened our mail box and found a card with a photo of his young daughter standing in the middle of a field of new spring flowers with her face and arms lifted towards the sun. On the back my friend had written, "Ron, at lunch I listened closely to what you said about Jesus and his love for me. I was so overwhelmed by this truth I could hardly talk. After I left you, I went for a walk on the beach. Somewhere between the restaurant and my beach house I invited Jesus to come into my heart as Lord and Savior." Experiences like this one continually motivate me to choose to allow the perfume of Jesus to flow out of me as I interact with others. I can trust God that his aroma will linger in their minds and hearts long after I have left the situation.

However, Paul says that two very different groups smell that fragrance of the knowledge of Christ. It comes first to "those who are being saved." In the triumphal procession these would have been healthy and useful slaves—cooks, household servants, administrators, etc.—who were taken to the slave markets to be sold, many of them eventually to be set free. In reality, the friend I just mentioned belonged to this group. For the first group the perfume of Jesus is a fragrance of life and freedom. For the second group, "those who are perishing," that same perfume of Jesus becomes a "smell of death." In the immediate first century context, the second group included the captured and humiliated kings and chieftains as well as the sick, rebellious, and aged. Following the parade, these people were taken to a tent and strangled. For them, the incense was literally the "smell of death."

On a recent trip to Germany and France, my wife and I met a very successful German businesswoman who was newly widowed. We invited her to dinner at our host's villa. All of us were having a wonderful evening together. Finally, she insisted on knowing my line of work, though I had been avoiding the topic for most of the meal. I looked her in the eye and said, "I tell people about Jesus Christ when they are interested. Are you interested?" She looked at me for a moment and then said in so many mocking words, "Why does anyone need Jesus Christ in this modern age?" The pleasant evening soon drew to a close, and she left. We have not heard from her since. Sadly, she may be in the group of those who are perishing, though the Lord may well have worked in her life since then.

Acceptable to God

Paul encourages us to choose to be thankful because our risen Lord is leading us in one spiritual victory after another, and to realize that he is using us like incense in our society. He then adds that the very perfume of Jesus in our lives also rises to God. We are totally acceptable before him because of our relationship with his Son, Jesus. That is great news. We who have placed our faith in Jesus as our Lord have had all our sins placed on him on the cross. We now stand in a forgiven state before the one and only living God. That is why we are acceptable to God. Paul wrote to the Romans, "Therefore there is now no condemnation for those who are in Christ Jesus ... because those who are led by the Spirit of God are sons of God. For you did not receive a spirit that makes you a slave again to fear, but you received the Spirit of sonship. And by him we cry, 'Abba, [daddy] Father.'"[20] God accepts us as his beloved children, and nothing can change that.

As Paul reflects on God's desire for us to live a life of thankfulness, triumph, influence and security in our relationship with him, he recognizes his inability to live this way. The apostle cries out, "Who is equal to such a task?" There are two reasons behind Paul's question. The first is the bent of our human nature to look at something like this list and say to ourselves, "I can keep that list of requirements." We can see this tendency clearly in the instance when God gave the Ten Commandments to Moses and asked him to take them to his people. When Moses told the people all the Lord's words and laws, they responded with one voice, "We will do everything the Lord has said; we will obey."[21] So God instructed Moses to sprinkle the people with the blood of their animal sacrifice as a symbol of the blood of the covenant as well as a symbol of forgiveness for their sin of self-confidence. (We'll explore this issue of self-confidence more fully in chapter 4.)

The other reason behind Paul's question stems from the trial that he and his disciples had experienced in Asia, which had prevented them from keeping their promise to visit the Corinthians.[22] He uses the lesson from this difficult and stressful event to unfold the mystery of Christlike living in a Christless society:

> We do not want you to be uninformed, brothers, about the hardships we suffered in the province of Asia. We were under great pressure, far beyond our ability to endure, so that we despaired even of life.

Indeed, in our hearts we felt the sentence of death. But this happened *that we might not rely on ourselves but on God*, who raises the dead. He has delivered us from such a deadly peril, and he will deliver us. On him we have set our hope that he will continue to deliver us.[23]

Like Paul, each one of us struggles with trusting Jesus fully. We need him to provide all the strength, power, wisdom, knowledge, courage and endurance to face each day's challenges. Some days we face a certain trial and we reach within ourselves for courage, but at the same time ask the Lord to provide the patience. Other days we face some stressful circumstance and find ourselves gathering information to protect ourselves, but may reach out to God for the wisdom to apply that knowledge to eliminate the stress. In the case of Paul, the Lord allowed him to come to the point where he had absolutely no physical or emotional resources left—no friends, no political power to get him out of these deadly circumstances, no inner strength left to endure, and no hope of getting out alive. As far as they could surmise, their hopes, dreams, and lives were over. Then somehow they were delivered from this horrible situation. In retrospect, Paul saw that he and his companions had learned that in every circumstance of life they were no longer to rely on themselves, but on God who raises the dead. It was only God who could take the most "deadly" of circumstances and give it life.

Integrity

The prevalent world-view of pragmatism encourages us, "If it works, do it!" This philosophy is unconcerned with ethics and moral precepts. In contrast, Paul sought to encourage the Corinthian Christian community that he and his companions were "not like many, peddling the word of God." False apostles had begun to water down the Scriptures, trying to make them more palatable to the Corinthians. Here Paul contrasts his Christ-centered ministry with their self-centered ministry and describes some characteristics of Christian integrity.

The foremost component of integrity is sincerity. In ancient times, Corinth was filled with potters who made wonderful clay pots to sell in the marketplace. If the firing process caused the pot to crack a bit, the potter would sometimes fill the crack with hot wax. When the wax cooled, he would paint over it and place the pot on the table outside his shop in the morning. By noon, however, the wax would begin to melt, and it would soon be evident that the pot was cracked and had been patched with wax; it was insincere. Paul says that he chooses to live his life by the power of God, resulting in a life of sincerity; literally, without wax. He was the genuine article.

Another key to Christian integrity is conscious accountability to God. "In Christ we speak before God," Paul says. We are not self-appointed, but ambassadors of Christ who speak his message with authority from him. When Paul began his letter to the Corinthians he wrote: "Paul, an apostle of Christ Jesus by the will of God." He did not choose this job; God chose him. When Saul (as he was then called) met the resurrected Jesus on a trip to Syria from Jerusalem with orders to imprison all the "followers of Jesus" he could find, he was blinded by the bright light of heaven and had to be led by the hand to a home in Damascus. While he waited, a Jewish believer named Ananias was told in a vision from the Lord to go visit him, lay his hands on him and restore his sight. Ananias was afraid, but Jesus said to him, "Go! This man is my chosen instrument to carry my name before the Gentiles and their kings and before the people of Israel."[24]

With this direct appointment from God, Paul clearly recognized his responsibility to speak God's words plainly and freely. He received no financial gain from this task—in fact, it involved a great deal of suffering! Paul says, "You Corinthians know that our life and strength come from the resurrected Jesus working through us. We are always conscious that God is watching us and listening to us. We seek to live and speak in awareness of his eternal power and presence."

A few years ago, our staff was invited to a pastors conference in Houston, Texas. One of the seminars was to be led by a well-known and greatly loved Christian leader, but he seemed to be running late. Finally he appeared on the platform before a large and admiring crowd. He looked awful—his suit was wrinkled, his eyes were bloodshot, his hair stuck up in places, and he needed a shave. As he stood before that crowd, we all waited to hear the story behind his harried and late arrival, which was completely out of character. I was sure this spiritual giant had become involved in some kind of spiritual warfare that had lasted all night, or a critical counseling situation that had caused him to lose track of time—but whatever the case, he was now here, faithful to the task of teaching us the Scriptures.

This was a perfect moment for him to fabricate some great excuse for being so late to the seminar. Instead, he told us the truth: He admitted that he had forgotten the meeting, but as soon as his secretary reminded him, he bought a ticket from Los Angeles to Houston. Unfortunately, the only flight available was the red-eye. Upon arrival that morning, he discovered that the airline had lost his luggage. He checked into his room, washed his face, and then realized that his Bible was in his luggage. He "borrowed" a Gideon Bible from the hotel room and caught a cab to the convention center. Then he said with a big smile, "So opening our Gideon Bibles, let's turn to ...." Here was a sincere man of God, a man who lived his daily life "without wax."

Summary

Our calling as disciples of Jesus Christ is to become more and more like him in a society that has rarely even heard of him, let alone seen him in the lives of his followers. God does not ask us to "try harder," but to come to the full realization that he has never asked us to do anything without first providing the necessary resources to accomplish what he has asked. The first resource we need to appropriate is the gift of the indwelling Holy Spirit. He alone will provide the power to develop a lifestyle of thankfulness even in the midst of our current stress.

He alone will enable us to trust him daily for spiritual victories over invisible spiritual foes. He has enabled us to become a sweet fragrance of Jesus to God our Father as well as to those around us who are either in the process of coming to know him as Lord or are rejecting him at the moment. Finally, the Spirit of God provides the power to live and work among our family and friends with integrity and a conscious awareness that we are always seeking to live in God's sight. As we shall see, our Lord Jesus will also provide forgiveness when we fail in any of these areas and then encourage us to trust him to begin again.

As I discussed earlier, we are now living in a "post-Christian" society. The forces in this age seek to include us in the shifting sands of their moral and spiritual values while rejecting the firm foundation of absolute truth that is found in Jesus Christ and his Word. The voices of the many self-help groups and the New Age movement promise relief from the stress of our tension-filled society by encouraging us to make ourselves winners, or by informing us we are gods. The Apostle Paul has shown us that peace of mind can come only from a personal relationship with the Prince of Peace.

Chapter 3

Free-at Last!
TO BE COMPETENT

"I can do everything through him who gives me strength."

- Paul[1]

Most of us long to be competent and self-sufficient, but find that life holds many overwhelming challenges. Statements like the following one from a self-help magazine grab our attention: "Man is made or unmade by himself. By the right choice he ascends. As a being of power, intelligence and love, and lord of his own thoughts, he holds the key to every situation." How I wish life were like that. Half the time, I can't even find the keys to my car!

These days, people in all walks of life are losing their jobs by the thousands. The sense of loss and discouragement is taking a heavy toll as so many try to find another job in their field or retrain for a totally new endeavor. Many of these men and women were very successful and well regarded in their former companies. Now for the first time in years, they must write a personal résumé and generate a list of references. They must face the stressful and humbling experience of interviewing with people who know nothing about them and have no appreciation for their past successes. These aspects of job hunting can easily make a person feel totally incompetent.

We now find the Apostle Paul in a position similar to that of the job-hunter, only more stressful. It is as if a young interviewer is insisting to see Paul's letters of recommendation before proceeding with the interview, even though Paul himself founded the "company" and trained all the present leaders.

God called Paul to preach the good news of Jesus Christ and establish new churches throughout the Roman world. He was to ensure that these groups of believers had good shepherds to care for them and lead them. Reflecting on the high calling of all Christians, Paul has just asked, "Who is equal to such a task?" Paul will now explain another spiritual secret to help us become competent to serve God and be filled with peace and joy.

Trust in the Work of the Holy Spirit

> Are we beginning to commend ourselves again?
> Or do we need, like some people, letters of
> recommendation to you or from you? You your-
> selves are our letter, written on our hearts, known
> and read by everybody. You show that you are a
> letter from Christ, the result of our ministry,
> written not with ink but with the Spirit of the
> living God, not on tablets of stone but on tablets
> of human hearts.[2]

In the midst of expressing his joy over the Corinthians' receptivity to his "painful letter," Paul stops and asks: Does it sound like we're bragging or trying to produce our credentials? Later in this letter he writes: "Let him who boasts, boast in the Lord. For it is not the one who commends himself who is approved, but the one whom the Lord commends."[3] Paul was clearly not trying to promote himself.

Paul then asks the elders of the Corinthian church if they expect him to produce references or use them as a reference. First-century travelers had to carry letters of recommendation with them whenever they left their own areas. This practice was quite common in the Christian community because of the number of false apostles who tried to infiltrate them. For example, Paul wrote such a letter for the men who carried the offering to Jerusalem during the famine.[4] Christians in Ephesus wrote a letter of introduction for Apollos when he traveled to various cities in Greece. Questioning Paul's apostolic authority, some of the false teachers had apparently suggested to the leaders of the Corinthian church that before they invited him back into their fellowship he should, like all *unknown* spiritual teachers, send them some letters of recommendation. But here Paul reminds them why he, Titus, and Timothy would never again need letters of introduction to visit the church in Corinth which they had helped establish some five years earlier.

First, he says, "You yourselves are our letter, written on our hearts..." We can discover what Paul means by this statement if we look at his earlier letter to the Corinthians.

> Do you not know that the wicked will not inherit the kingdom of God? Do not be deceived: Neither the sexually immoral nor idolaters nor adulterers nor male prostitutes nor homosexual offenders nor thieves nor the greedy nor drunkards nor slanderers nor swindlers will inherit the kingdom of God. And that is what some of you were. But you were washed, you were sanctified, you were justified in the name of the Lord Jesus Christ and by the Spirit of our God.[5]

Why would Paul and his associates need letters of recommendation to the Corinthian church when the Corinthians themselves were living testimony to the work of the Holy Spirit through the apostle's life and teaching? They could not deny the reality of their own changed lives. Though they were once flagrant sinners, they had been made righteous in Christ, and the memory of that transformation was etched on the apostle's heart.

They were "known and read by everybody." Their families and friends experienced the difference that Christ had made in their lives. These Corinthians used to be drunkards, thieves, and so on, but they had been washed, sanctified and justified in Christ. Their changed lifestyle was as evident as an open book. Paul didn't need a letter of recommendation; all he needed to do was point to his first-hand knowledge of their transformation.

I recently visited a man who is battling a serious form of cancer. When I entered his hospital room, I found his wife helping him take some medication. Here was an interesting couple: They had both professed to be Christians, but for various reasons they left their former spouses to marry each other. After a few years of marriage, they both became convicted of their sins and confessed them before God, their children and parents, and former mates. A wonderful spiritual healing had taken place, even to the point that this ailing man was able to lead his elderly father to the Lord.

During our visit, this man was dreaming about the day when he would recover. He said, "Wouldn't it be wonderful if one Sunday all of us could share with the church how God has healed us physically, emotionally and spiritually?" His wife replied that it would be hard to stand up and tell the church that she and her husband were adulterers. The way she said this made it sound like she believed that they were *still* adulterers. I handed her my Bible, asked her to read the Corinthian passage, and emphasized, "And such *were* some of you, *but* you were washed..." It is true that they were adulterers, but because of their confession to Christ Jesus as their Lord and sin-bearer, that which they *were* is gone. Now they are "new creatures in Christ." Thank God that the same truth applies to all of us who have given our lives to Jesus Christ!

A few years ago, I was invited to speak at the seventy-fifth anniversary of the orphanage where I lived from age twelve to nineteen. I had to double-check the invitation to make sure it was for me. When I left "the home" to join the Air Force, no one organized a good-bye party for me. In fact, two large staff members threw me out and told me never to come back.

I felt a lot of stress during the anniversary events because one of my best friends from high school had also been invited. As teenagers, he and I had caused many problems for the home and our high school. We were always in trouble with the authorities and had a bitter experience with Christianity in those days. My friend went on to become a very successful businessman, marry a Christian woman and have several children, but he continued to struggle with "religion."

During the three days of the celebration, I had the privilege of speaking on three occasions. Each time, my old buddy sat in the back of the auditorium, "reading" me. I wondered over and over if he were seeing the old me or if he had seen something new about me. I prayed, "Lord, please let him see *you* in me. The old me is dead. I'm a new creature. Let him see that." After the last session, my friend slowly approached me, looked me directly in the eyes for what seemed like several minutes, and finally said, "Ritchie, it's real." Then he walked away. He hadn't seen a perfect man, but a man in the process of becoming like Jesus. He had seen enough to convince him that I had been forgiven and changed by the Lord Jesus.

Similarly, Paul reminds the Corinthians that they "show that [they] are a letter from Christ." In other words, when others observed their lives, they clearly saw characteristics of Jesus. That is why Paul could say in Galatians, "I have been crucified with Christ and I no longer live, but Christ lives in me. The life I live in the body, I live by faith in the Son of God, who loved me and gave himself for me."[6]

The Corinthian Christians had also become the "fruit" of the apostle's ministry. He had been tempted to leave the city because of pressure from the Jews, but the Lord appeared to him in a vision and told him, "Do not be afraid; keep on speaking, do not be silent. For I am with you, and no one is going to attack and harm you, because I have many people in this city."[7] The apostle stayed for a year and a half, teaching them the word of God, and pouring his life into them. They knew each other well!

As a result of Paul's time teaching them God's word, the Corinthians themselves had become a letter from Christ, "written not with ink but with the Spirit of the living God, not on tablets of stone but on tablets of human hearts." They became letters of Christ because of the power of the Holy Spirit.

In 1989, James Hudson Taylor III discovered the tombstone of his great-grandfather, J. Hudson Taylor, pioneer missionary to China, in the cluttered storage yard of a museum in Zhenjiang. The graveyard where it stood had been razed years earlier, and local believers had tried to have the stone mounted at another site. Permission was granted, but the museum director demanded that the believers pay for twenty-six years of storage, which amounted to some thirteen thousand dollars. Pastors in China overseeing the restoration project informed the curator that he could keep the grave marker. In their letter they said that what was etched in the hearts of people as a result of the ministry of the revered missionary was more valuable than what was written on stone.[8]

The lives of these Corinthians had been changed by the Spirit of the living God. In reality, Paul did only one thing—he showed up in Corinth. That is what the Lord wants us to do—*just show up* and he will have the Holy Spirit function in us and through us to his honor and glory and our complete peace and joy.

The Work of the Holy Spirit

It is important at this point to remember the role that the Holy Spirit plays in the lives of the disciples of Jesus Christ. The Holy Spirit has a ministry of *conviction*. The Spirit works through believers to convict the world of sin, righteousness, and judgment. He does so by placing the truth of the gospel in a clear light before unbelievers so that it is acknowledged as truth whether they receive Christ or not.[9]

Another work of the Holy Spirit is *regeneration*. Faith is the human requirement that enables the Holy Spirit to give new life, eternal life. The word of God provides the content for faith. It's not faith in faith, but faith in Jesus as Lord and Savior as revealed in his spoken and written word. A few years later, Paul's disciple Titus would write:

> At one time we too were foolish, disobedient, deceived and enslaved by all kinds of passions and pleasures. We lived in malice and envy, being hated and hating one another. But when the kindness and love of God our Savior appeared, he saved us, not because of righteous things we had done, but because of his mercy. He saved us through the washing of rebirth and renewal by the Holy Spirit, whom he poured out on us generously through Jesus Christ our Savior, so that, having been justified by his grace, we might become heirs having the hope of eternal life.[10]

At a recent men's retreat sponsored by our church, a friend of mine introduced me to a middle-aged man originally from India. "Are you a Christian or are you in the process of becoming one?" I found myself asking him. He replied, "I am in the process of becoming one! My friend is helping me understand who Jesus Christ is by sharing the Scriptures and his life with me." The next afternoon as I was driving out of the parking lot, my friend and his Indian guest walked up to my Jeep and I could tell what they were going to say by the smiles on their faces. I rolled down the window and the first words out of my friend's mouth were, "Ron, I want you to meet a new brother in Jesus Christ." The evening before, because of the love of my friend, his knowledge of the Word of God, and the conviction of the Holy Spirit, this wonderful Indian invited Jesus to become his Lord and Savior. He was *regenerated*, born again spiritually by the power of the Holy Spirit, and became a son of God.[11]

The Holy Spirit also *indwells* believers. "Do you not know that your body is a temple of the Holy Spirit, who is in you, whom you have received from God? You are not your own; you were bought at a price. Therefore honor God with your body."[12] Believers are given the gift of the Holy Spirit, whose ministry in their life is to empower them for living, enable them for good works and service, and purge their motives and actions—all of this in order that Christ may be honored and praised. As believers learn to draw on God's power, this indwelling produces a Christlikeness which brings honor to him. Many Christians are so excited about the Holy Spirit working in them that they draw attention to themselves. The Holy Spirit is not meant to honor Christians, however, but to honor Christ, who in turn honors his Father in heaven.

The moment that a person personally invites Jesus Christ to become his Lord and Savior, the Holy Spirit *baptizes*, or places them into the spiritual body of Christ along with all the other believers who have established the same personal relationship since the day of Pentecost in 33 AD. Paul had already written the Corinthians and said, "The body is a unit, though it is made up of many parts; and though all its parts are many, they form one body. So it is with Christ. For we were all baptized by one Spirit into one body—whether Jews or Greeks, slave or free—and we were all given the one Spirit to drink."[13] Christians then acknowledge that spiritual reality by being physically baptized with water.

Finally, God *seals* his relationship to Christians with the Holy Spirit.

> You also were included in Christ when you heard
> the word of truth, the gospel of your salvation.
> Having believed, you were marked in him with a
> seal, the promised Holy Spirit, who is a deposit
> guaranteeing our inheritance until the redemption
> of those who are God's possession—to the praise
> of his glory.[14]

We can't get out of our relationship with God. Once when my younger son became upset with me, he said he was going to go to Africa, change his name and never come home. I told him that if he could afford to do it one day, he was certainly free to go to Africa, change his name and live in the darkest jungle. I assured him, though, that he would still know in his heart that he was my son, and that I would always love him no matter where he went under another name. It's the same with our Heavenly Father. The Holy Spirit seals Christians so that they will always be God's children.

Back to the Question

Paul learned the answer to his question, "Who is equal to such a task?"—the task of living a life of thankfulness to God who always leads us in triumph, spreads through us the fragrance of Christ, and finds us acceptable because we are hidden in Christ. How can we as Christians gain a godly sense of competence to be able to function on earth as God intended? Paul learned to trust the Holy Spirit in his own life, and then trust the Holy Spirit in the lives of the Corinthians. We too can gain a godly sense of competence, not in *our* talents, gifts or ministries, but by trusting in the person and power of the Holy Spirit.

My wife and I, for example, were invited to speak on the topic of marriage to the student body at a Christian college. We were intimidated at the prospect of facing a thousand students and being honest with them. We wondered why we had ever accepted the engagement.

When I look back on our marriage, I often wonder how my wife put up with me. I had no family to model after; I had no father to guide me; I had no spiritual heritage; and I came from an Italian culture that promoted man as king, and woman as servant without rights or privilege. In other words, I came to the wedding banquet very late and most of the food was already gone. My only hope was in the Lord himself, his Word and some dear older Christians friends who, without really knowing it, modeled a biblical marriage relationship for me. But Anne Marie and I learned to trust our Lord in those difficult years. Now as we look back over some four decades, we marvel at the grace of God on our behalf. We are now experiencing a love that I believe the Lord wanted us to enjoy for him and for each other from the very beginning of our relationship.

On the morning of the first session I was really nervous. We prayed, "Lord, you have brought us this far. We believe you are going to function through us. We want your Spirit to flow through us because we have no sense of competence or adequacy." We were set free to be totally honest about our struggles as well as our blessings. To the honor and glory of our Lord, the people at the college said it was a wonderful week of spiritual encouragement. That's the way he wants us to live, not just on special occasions as I have mentioned, but day by day, moment by moment.

Paul's sense of competence to live and minister came from trusting the Spirit of Christ to change and protect the lives of his spiritual family in Corinth even during his absence. Now he will go on to show that his confidence also comes from trusting in the work of his Heavenly Father.

Trust in the Power of God

> Such confidence as this is ours through Christ before God. Not that we are competent in ourselves to claim anything for ourselves, but our competence comes from God. He has made us competent as ministers of a new covenant—not of the letter but of the Spirit; for the letter kills, but the Spirit gives life.[15]

We return to the question, Who is equal to the task of living as God intends? "Such confidence as this is ours through Christ before God," Paul responds. In Paul's letter to the Christians in Philippi, Greece, we discover where the apostle got his confidence before he became a Christian. As Paul looked back on his religious upbringing and contrasted it with his new relationship with the Lord, he saw that his entire religious lifestyle had initiated within himself. He had depended on *his* personality, *his* wisdom, *his* strength, *his* courage, *his* knowledge, *his* family, *his* college experience and his ability to keep the law, never having called out to God to enable him to live his life to please the One who created him.[16] Once he met the risen Messiah on the road to Damascus, he began to realize that the Lord wanted him to come to him for everything necessary to live his new life. He began to see that there was a difference between living his life in his own strength or the strength of his hew Lord.

Then where did Paul get his sense of competence after his salvation? He tells us in these verses: "Not that we are competent in ourselves to claim anything for ourselves, but our competence comes from God." The secret of his life and ministry was a total dependence on God functioning through him. We normally think that if we give up using our self-confidence, talent, skills, personality and strength, we will be left empty and helpless. But Paul says, No! The moment we declare ourselves inadequate for the task set before us and choose to call on God, he immediately fills us with his total adequacy, wisdom, strength, knowledge and love. The apostle affirmed, "I can do everything through [Christ] who gives me strength."[17]

Further, he declares, "God has made us competent as ministers of a new covenant." A covenant is an agreement between two parties designed to regulate their relationship. A covenant may be a last will and testament directing the disposition of one's earthly goods upon one's death. A covenant may be an arrangement by one party with unilateral authority and power which the other party may accept or break, but not change. The key word here is "arrangement." The *new covenant* is an arrangement by God for living with his people, a unilateral agreement with authority and power which we may accept or break, but cannot change. God made several such arrangements with his people Israel. He made covenants with Adam, Noah, Abraham, Israel and David so that they could live in a right relationship with him.

The Old Covenant

In the context of this passage we are going to look at two of these covenants. "Old covenant" is a phrase contrasted by implication with the phrase "new covenant." The old covenant was the law that God handed to Moses on Mount Sinai. The Ten Commandments and accompanying regulations revealed God's character and how he desired his people to live. In the gospel of Luke, a rich young lawyer asked Jesus, "Teacher, what must I do to inherit eternal life?" Jesus said, "What is written in the Law?" He answered, "Love the Lord your God with all your heart and with all your soul and with all your strength and with all your mind; and 'Love your neighbor as yourself.'" And Jesus replied, "Do this, and you will live,"[18] realizing that no one could.

Paul also recognized this truth, referring to the old covenant as the "ministry that brought death" and the "ministry that condemns men."[19] Once it was given to the people of Israel, it "killed their spirit," because no man or woman in their own strength was ever able to live up to God's character and moral laws. The law in fact was designed to drive us to the grace of God as revealed in his Son Jesus Christ, who shed his blood on the cross so God could forgive our sins. Paul would write to the Roman Christians about the Law:

> Is the law sin? Certainly not! Indeed I would not have known what sin was except through the law. For I would not have known what coveting really was if the law had not said, "Do not covet." But sin, seizing the opportunity afforded by the commandment, produced in me every kind of covetous desire.... I found that the very commandment that was intended to bring life actually brought death.... So then, the law is holy, and the commandment is holy, righteous and good.[20]

So the law of God—the old covenant—is holy, righteous and good, but God never intended for us to keep it in our own power. Rather, God gave the law to show us his awesome character and how far we fall short of what he created us to be. This in turn places us in a position of spiritual bankruptcy before God, causing us to cry out to him for his mercy, love, grace and power to live a life pleasing to him. This is where the *"new covenant"* of God comes in.

The New Covenant

The new covenant was an arrangement that God made with Israel following the seventy-year Babylonian captivity between 600 and 500 BC. It is mentioned in Ezekiel,[21] Isaiah,[22] and as we shall see below, Jeremiah. Jeremiah starts off with a statement of future hope for the nation of Israel when they will finally come into the land after the great tribulation. They will serve Jesus, who will sit on the throne of David and reign in righteousness for a thousand years. God declares, "The time is coming … when I will make a new covenant with the house of Israel and with the house of Judah."

Then he refers to the *old covenant*: "It will not be like the covenant I made with their forefathers when I took them by the hand to lead them out of Egypt, because they broke my covenant, though I was a husband to them."

And here is the content of the new covenant:

> "This is the covenant I will make with the house of Israel after that time," declares the Lord. "I will put my law in their minds and write it on their hearts. I will be their God, and they will be my people. No longer will a man teach his neighbor, or a man his brother, saying, 'Know the Lord,'

because they will all know me, from the least of
them to the greatest," declares the Lord. "For I
will forgive their wickedness, and will remember
their sins no more."[23]

The books of the Old Testament were originally written in
Hebrew, and the books and letters of the New Testament were
originally written in Greek. The word "new" in Hebrew and
Greek does not mean brand-new, but renewed, restated, fresh, or
better in quality, yet not necessarily later in time. God has always
had a "new" covenant with his people. He has always wanted man
to live by faith in him, relying on his strength and wisdom. The
writer of Hebrews calls it the *eternal covenant*,[24] the arrangement
God has always wanted to have with his people in every generation since the creation of Adam and Eve.

The new covenant that God initiated with Israel as a nation will
be fulfilled to the letter when Jesus comes to earth again as King
of Kings and Lord of Lords and establishes his Kingdom. Until
then, individual Jews and Gentiles alike can enjoy the *spiritual*
blessings of that covenant *now*. Jesus offered the new covenant to
the Jewish nation during his earthly ministry, but they rejected it.
So on the evening before his crucifixion, he gathered his disciples
(individual Jews) around him. He lifted up a cup of wine before
them and said, "This cup is the new covenant [the same words
used in Jeremiah and Ezekiel] in my blood, which is poured out
for you."[25] The next day his blood was shed. The church—his
disciples then and in every generation to follow—was then to
experience *spiritually* all the new covenant blessings promised to
Israel.

Here is how David Roper described this new covenant in his
book, *The New Covenant In The Old Testament*: "The new covenant
was a restatement of the basic eternal arrangement for maintaining a living, loving relationship between God and man. As we cast
our lot with him and lay hold of his life, he will increasingly
bestow on us his power for obedience and his forgiveness for

weakness and failure."[26] On the night before his death, Jesus explained the essence of the new covenant in these words: "I am the vine, you are the branches.... Apart from me you can do nothing."[27] The new covenant is, "It is no longer I who live, but Christ who lives in me." The new covenant is everything coming from God, nothing from us. It is total dependence on Christ for the power to cope with reality. The result is peace, joy and wholeness in the Holy Spirit.

The Old Covenant vs. the New Covenant

Now Paul contrasts the old covenant with the new covenant, hoping to show the Corinthians the glory of the new covenant.

> Now if the ministry that brought death, which was engraved in letters on stone, came with glory, so that the Israelites could not look steadily at the face of Moses because of its glory, fading though it was, will not the ministry of the Spirit be even more glorious?[28]

Paul has in mind Jews who have become Christians but were being tempted to put themselves back under the law. "Now if that ministry [of the law] brought death...," he says. The law condemned man. It produced death and killed the spirit because man found he could not keep the requirements of the law. As I have said, many people think that Christianity is just a matter of obeying a different set of laws than the ones which they have set as a standard for themselves—and failed to keep! But humanity was never designed to keep the law.

The Christian and Jewish communities are not the only ones having trouble living up to the letter of the law. The Moslem community also struggles to live up to the standards of its law, the Koran. On a recent trip to Israel, my friends and I were visiting the Temple Mount when a delightful middle-aged Arab approached and asked us if we would like him to guide us on a tour around the Mount. He also offered to take us into the Dome of the Rock, the sacred building which was built by Caliph Omar over the site of Solomon's temple in the seventh century BC. We agreed, and once we took off our shoes, he began to share the teaching of Islam and the obligation placed on each Moslem to fulfill the five pillars of their faith. Moslems must recite the Kalima: There is no god but God and Mohammed is his prophet. They must also recite prayers from the Koran five times daily in Arabic, while facing toward Mecca. They must fast during the month of Ramadan and give a compulsory percentage of the property they own to the poor. Finally, all Moslems are required to make a pilgrimage to Mecca once in their lifetime.

In the course of our conversation, I asked him what determined his hope to be taken to heaven when he died. He said that no Moslem can be sure he will go to heaven, but that each has a choice whether to follow the teachings of the Koran. No one is perfect, so each life will be placed in the balance, he said, and he is hoping that he will be found acceptable in the eyes of God. At the moment, like all his fellow Moslems, he is not sure if he will get into heaven. Many Christians and Jews who live under the law are also not quite sure if they have kept enough of it to be accepted in the sight of God, but most hope they have. What a terrible burden! No matter what religion one serves, "the letter kills" because none of us has any sustaining power to keep it.

Although it came with the glory of a consuming fire on Mount Sinai, the old covenant brought death to the spirit.[29] But it was a fading glory. I was raised in a religion that had a lot of glory about it. A few years ago, I took my elderly mother-in-law to her church and waited while she completed an elaborate ritual. As I stood there I remembered how as a boy, I thought it was glorious, especially on Palm Sunday and Easter. But I would never dream of going back to it in exchange for all I have now in Jesus Christ and his indwelling Spirit because I have seen something much more glorious. Once I felt guilty all the time because I could not keep up with all the laws which that religion imposed on me. But the glory of it kept fading until I finally avoided going to church except at Christmas and Easter.

Paul draws a second contrast between the old and new covenants:

> If the ministry that condemns men is glorious,
> how much more glorious is the ministry
> that brings righteousness! For what was .
> glorious has no glory now in comparison with
> the surpassing glory.[30]

The law is glorious because it reflects the character of God, but it condemns because it offers the person who understands it no power to keep it. But the ministry that brings righteousness allows us to stand before God forever without condemnation. The law once had a certain glory. However, now that God has established a relationship with us, his new covenant has a surpassing glory. It is the difference between the glory of looking at a photograph of the Grand Canyon and the glory of experiencing it in person. In the same way, Paul is saying that the glory of the old covenant, the ministry of condemnation, faded in the light of the new covenant, the ministry of righteousness.

"And if what was fading away came with glory, how much greater is the glory of that which lasts!"[31] The old covenant was fading away. It was temporary, a shadow of what was to come. But the new covenant is lasting, better, and eternal, because the Spirit, not the law, is at the center of it.

Freedom to be Competent

How can we find the freedom to be competent to live on this earth as God intended us to live? We need to trust in the work of the Holy Spirit. Paul's sense of competence to live and minister came from trusting in the Holy Spirit to act in the lives of believers in Corinth. So we also must trust in the person, the presence and the power of the Holy Spirit, moment by moment, until we join our Lord in eternity. Then, like Jesus in his resurrection state, we will continue to rely on the Holy Spirit forever.[32] Not only is he at work maturing us, but he is also at work through us convicting the world of sin as well as regenerating, indwelling, baptizing and sealing the lives of new believers in this generation.

We must also trust in the power of our Heavenly Father. Our sense of competence to cope with earthly and spiritual reality does not come from self-effort, self-reliance or self-confidence. Our competence comes from God our Heavenly Father. Through the shed blood of his Son Jesus Christ he has provided a new, fresh restatement of the basic eternal arrangement for maintaining our relationship with him. We can trust him to provide the strength to obey him and to forgive our weakness and failure.

One of the best illustrations of this spiritual principle comes from the life of Moses. The story of the burning bush has always brought a smile to my lips. God appeared to Moses and asked him to go to Egypt and deliver his people from their four hundred years of bondage. Moses had been a murderer on the run for some forty years and was not about to return to the nation that featured his face on the most-wanted list in every post office. So Moses tried to persuade God that he was incompetent to appear before Pharaoh and deliver a message from God.

> Moses said to the Lord, "O Lord, I have never been eloquent, neither in the past nor since you have spoken to your servant. I am slow of speech and tongue." The Lord said to him, "Who gave man his mouth? Who makes him deaf or mute? Who gives him sight or makes him blind? Is it not I, the Lord? Now go [show up!]; I will help you speak and will teach you what to say."[33]

There is the heart of the new covenant. *Just show up*—in your neighborhood, at work, in all your relationships—and allow God to work and speak through you. He will make you competent as a minister of the new covenant, as you trust him to provide everything you will ever need to please him.

Chapter 4

Free at Last!

TO BE TRANSPARENT

The man who loves God is known by God.

- Paul[1]

Below is an excerpt from a poem published in a Young Life magazine several years ago. The anonymous author shows great insight into the tendency we all have to hide behind a mask. This modern poem has a lot to say about the subject we will be addressing in this next section of Paul's letter to his Corinthian family.

Please Hear What I'm Not Saying

Don't be fooled by me.
Don't be fooled by the face I wear
For I wear a mask,
I wear a thousand masks, masks I'm afraid to take off.
And none of them are me.

Pretending is an art that's second nature with me,
But don't be fooled,
For God's sake don't be fooled.

I give you the impression that I'm secure,
That all is sunny and unruffled with me,
Within as well as without;

That confidence is my name and coolness my game,
That the water's calm and I'm in command,
And that I need no one.
But don't believe me, please.

Indeed, so many people play a part, hiding behind a variety of masks. They fear rejection if anyone finds out who they really are inside. Unfortunately, the problem of hiding behind masks has penetrated the Christian community on a grand scale. It has done great harm to the individuals involved, as well as to the church and the community at large.

This "game playing" was a natural part of our old life before we came into a spiritual relationship with Jesus Christ. The temptation to keep playing the game of "make believe" as a Christian is very hard to overcome for the same reason the poet stated—the fear of rejection. To add to the problem, as we look around the Christian community, we falsely believe that some older Christians are almost perfect and would be greatly disappointed to learn how weak we are. What we fail to realize is that many of those "older" Christians are still hiding behind their own masks. This hiding is what keeps all of us from living transparently before God and each other. That is why so often when we are asked, "How are you?" we choose to respond with safe answers like, "Just fine, thanks for asking. And how are you?" All the while we are hurting inside from some spiritual failure or emotional pain that won't go away. Too often, they don't even crack open the door as we hear them answer our question, "Just fine, thanks. Listen, I have to go now. You know, I'm just so busy these days with the choir and the children and the sports activities and…!"

There is a great need for transparency in the Christian community. Our wonderful Lord Jesus has called us to live our lives without any masks in our society. The temptation to be someone we are not arises from our old life, that is, the life we lived before we asked Christ to become our new master. In our old life, we did not know who we were, so we took our cues on how to play different parts from the society around us. The temptation in our new life arises when we no longer believe that "our adequacy is from God, who also made us adequate as servants of a new covenant." At that moment of doubt, we find ourselves being lured into a world of fantasies, some of which we have created ourselves, and others which the society around us has created, calling out to us to join them in their masquerade ball.

You can see the mask some husbands wear when you hear them telling others how much they love their wife, yet joking in the locker room about lusting for their female co-workers. You can see the mask some mothers wear when they talk of their commitment to their children, yet are never available when the children need them. You can suspect the game is being played when one of your friends displays a high intolerance for the sins of others, but seems unaware of his own shortcomings. You can really sense the game is being played when you find your own heart filled with self-righteousness as you criticize the weaknesses of everyone you meet.

The Scriptures call that hypocrisy. A hypocrite is one who pretends to be someone he is not, plays a part, or pretends to be better than he is. In contrast to our old nature—the life we lived before we met Jesus—we now seek to allow the Holy Spirit to teach us how to live sincere, transparent lives in this masked society. We need this transparency so that the sweet fragrance of Jesus may flow freely out of our lives into the community in which we live, offering the hope of eternal life to everyone around us who wants it.

The apostle Paul sought to encourage the Christian community in Corinth to live "with unveiled faces" in their masked society. He uses two familiar negative examples to arrest their attention and then reminds them of the secret of maintaining a lifestyle of godly transparency.

We Are Not Like Moses

> Therefore, since we have such a hope, we are very
> bold. We are not like Moses, who would put a veil
> over his face to keep the Israelites from gazing at
> it while the radiance was fading away.[2]

Paul was not placing his hope in hope itself. In spite of his challenging circumstances, he was placing his hope in the one and only living God who raises the dead.[3] Further, his hope was based on the promises of God. God had promised that if Paul would place his faith in him, he would make him a competent servant of the new covenant. The apostle's hope was that God by his Spirit would provide all that he needed to cope with his present realities.

Finally set free from the burden of trying to keep the law of God in his own power, Paul continued to choose to live his new life in Christ in the power of the Holy Spirit. He discovered a new boldness in his ministry. As a minister of the new covenant, he found he was free to speak without fear; he was confident, open, and transparent in the sight of God and the Corinthians. He did not need letters of recommendation. This spiritual boldness came out of a thankful heart. It was not rudeness, but an ability to tell the truth in love, to preach the word of God in all kinds of circumstances without shame, to be open in his dealings with others within the Christian church as well as the surrounding community. He had the freedom to live without masks. Paul was bold because his sins had been forgiven by Christ's death on the cross; he was reconciled to God through Christ; God's law was written on his heart by the Holy Spirit; and he had personal access to and knowledge of God. The apostle was personally experiencing the truths of the new covenant spoken through God's prophet Jeremiah,[4] as we discussed in the previous chapter. Living within the promises of the new covenant means we are willing to go to God for all the resources we will need in any given day, for any given circumstance, with the realization that he hears us and is willing to meet our current need. It is a lifestyle modeled after the Lord Jesus when he prayed to God on the night before his death, "not my will, but yours be done."[5]

Paul then contrasts himself and his disciples with Moses, "who would put a veil over his face to keep the Israelites from gazing at it while the radiance was fading away." He has already explained part of the reason that Moses had to wear a veil: "The Israelites could not look steadily at the face of Moses because of its glory, fading though it was."[6] The glory of God and his law were reflected in Moses' face, but that brilliance was *fading*. The Old Testament passages will tell us the rest of the story.

God gave the law to Moses two times. The first time,[7] the law came with great glory. God descended on Mount Sinai in a dense cloud of smoke and fire. Trumpets blasted and the mountain quaked violently. Forty days and forty nights later, God gave the law, written on stone tablets, to Moses. But when he came down from the mountain ready to share with the Israelites the heart of God written in the law, he found the people worshipping a golden statue of a calf. Moses broke the tablets in anger over this idolatry.[8]

Now let's look at the second giving of the law. Moses had asked God if he could behold his glory. God told him that no man could behold him and live, but he allowed Moses to see his back as he passed by. Then God gave him the law again, and forty days later...

> When Moses came down from Mount Sinai with
> the two tablets of the Testimony in his hands, he
> was not aware that his face was radiant because
> he had spoken with the Lord. When Aaron and
> all the Israelites saw Moses, his face was radiant,
> and they were afraid to come near him. But
> Moses called to them; so Aaron and all the lead-
> ers of the community came back to him, and he

spoke to them. Afterward all the Israelites came
near him, and he gave them all the commands the
Lord had given him on Mount Sinai.

When Moses finished speaking to them, he put a
veil over his face. But whenever he entered the
Lord's presence to speak with him, he removed
the veil until he came out. And when he came out
and told the Israelites what he had been commanded, they saw that his face was radiant. Then
Moses would *put the veil back over his face* until he
went in to speak with the Lord.[9]

   In his letter, Paul points out something not recorded in Exodus.
Moses wore the veil longer than necessary, long after the glory
of God reflected on his face had faded. Why? Perhaps he feared
losing the respect of the Israelites and his authority over them.
During the wilderness journey, the Israelites were very stubborn
and difficult to lead. Moses realized that as long as he wore the
veil, the people showed him respect because they believed that he
was still visiting God. Otherwise, why would he keep the veil on?
But when Moses had not been in the presence of God, the glory
of God began to fade underneath the veil and he feared that if he
took off the veil, the people would get out of control again. He
wasn't transparent about his fading glory; he hid it. The glory,
power, and authority belonged to the Lord, not to Moses, and
God's glory never fades. Moses' face merely reflected the glory
of God when he was in God's glorious presence.

   We can understand Moses' problem in light of the typical
Christian retreat experience. I have attended countless retreats
over the years, and they are usually spiritual "highs." That is,
retreats are times when we can step back from the world we live
in, meet with other friends in a scenic setting and spend several
days having fun singing, studying God's word and enjoying time
together. In the closing message, the speaker usually says something like, "Well, now we all have to go off this mountain and
head down into the real world, so let me pray for you." We pack

our bags, sing all the new songs we learned, and review our notes from the messages. Before we know it, we are back home and the realities of this world immediately set in. A few weeks later, we may meet a friend who attended the same retreat and we feel a kindred spirit. We put on our camp "veil," but something is missing. We use the same words, but the life and power they had has been weakened. We hunger for the same relationship, but everyone is so busy. Slowly we begin to realize that the real reason we sense a fading glory is that we have not been in the presence of the Lord for the last two weeks. We have been living off the spirit of a fading retreat memory.

The Definition of a Veil

What does the veil represent in the context of Paul's letter? In the case of Moses, the veil represented a false sense of competence, power and authority, which he used to cover his fear and inadequacy in leading the Israelites. As long as he was living in the presence of God and drawing on his glory to speak God's words, there was no need for the veil. After he left the presence of God, however, fear entered his heart and he sought in his own strength to represent the glory that had faded from his face. But Paul says that he and his fellow-workers are not like Moses. They were sincere in discussing the gospel.

I have had to learn this lesson many times in my own life. I still struggle with the temptation to "put on my veil" when I become afraid or sense that I am not adequate. Let me share with you a situation which the Lord used to drive this point home. As a young man just out of graduate school, I had become a pastor at a church in Northern California. Within my first year, I was asked to become a representative for a Christian publishing company because our church was using their material. This position opened the door for me to travel around the country to promote their material at area conferences. On one of my first trips, I found myself sitting next to a businesswoman, and for two hours we discussed a variety of subjects.

Finally, as the crew told us to fasten our seatbelts for landing, this very pleasant woman asked, "What do you do for a living?" (I can still feel the pressure on the back of my neck as I think of this story.) "I'm a teacher," I answered. "What subjects do you teach?" she inquired. "Literature." She apparently had a great interest in literature so she pressed, "What period of literature?" I was really being trapped in a corner of my own making and weakly replied, "Sixteenth century," (meaning I taught out of the sixteenth century King James Bible). There was a long silence as she looked out the window of the plane. Then she abruptly turned to me and said, "You're a preacher, aren't you?" I looked down at the floor. "Yes," I admitted. Her next words have never left my heart. With some disappointment in her voice, she asked, "Why didn't you say so in the first place?"

Well, I knew why I had not said so in the first place. I enjoyed being in an intelligent conversation with this woman for over two hours without ever talking about the gospel of Jesus Christ. I thought that if I did talk about him, she might reject me. That was such a difficult lesson to learn, but I have asked the Lord Jesus since that day to give me the boldness to speak by his power and not to be ashamed of his name. Since that time, I have gotten into countless conversations with strangers, knowing that at some point they are going to ask me, "So, what do you do for a living?" I find myself now praying to the Lord each time someone asks me. Having considered the setting, I ask for his boldness to respond firmly and kindly with one of the following answers, and sometimes both: "I love to tell people about Jesus Christ when they are interested. Are you interested in talking about him?" Or, "I am a follower of Jesus Christ who has called me to be a pastor within a local community." My job title gives me a quick opening to talk about Jesus, which I realize is not the case for most people. I want to encourage you, though, to use every opportunity to share your relationship with Christ openly and honestly.

Jesus Christ calls his followers to choose to live their lives not as their fantasies would invite, nor as they would like others to think they live, but transparently in the power of the Holy Spirit. When we choose to live transparently as a lifestyle, then the world can see that Jesus Christ is in full control of our lives. In this way his love is able to freely flow from us like a sweet-smelling perfume, offering the hope of salvation to those who are in the process of being saved. We choose _not_ to be like Moses, who wore a veil out of fear, to hide the fading glory of God. We can also choose not to be like another group that is wearing veils, the self-righteous religious community.

The Self-Righteous

> But their minds were made dull, for to this day the same veil remains when the old covenant is read. It has not been removed, because only in Christ is it taken away. Even to this day when Moses is read, a veil covers their hearts.[10]

Now Paul shifts his focus from Moses to the sons of Israel. When the Israelites heard Moses recite the law of God in the wilderness, their hearts were filled with pride. "We can do it," they said.[11] They could not see that the law, good and glorious as it was in revealing the heart of God, could only be fulfilled in the power of the Lord. These dear people, however, wanted to cling to the law and try to keep it in their own strength. They hoped to gain personal salvation by keeping the law.

At the time that Paul was writing to the Corinthians, he remembered the Jews who lived and worshipped in the city of Corinth. He reminded the new Christians from the Jewish community that over the hundreds of years since the law had been given to Moses, each new generation had been tempted to read it and immediately say in their hearts, "I can do it in my own strength." This attitude had dulled their minds to the spiritual reality that they were never asked to keep the law in their own strength, but to rely on the Lord to keep it.

There is a certain glory and joy in trying to keep the Ten Commandments. But with that glory come a blinding pride, a self-righteous heart, and hateful contempt for those who don't measure up. Yet those who hold contempt for their spiritual brothers can't see their own failure, their own fading glory. If they could, their hearts would be filled with shame and despair, followed by spiritual and emotional weariness and death. When the Israelites said they could obey the law, God said to Moses, "Oh, that their hearts would be inclined to fear me and keep all my commands always, so that it might go well with them and their children forever!"[12] They tried to obey by relying on their own strength, and over time God caused their minds to become dull so that they could not even think about what they were doing. They placed a veil of pride over their hearts, which blinded them to the reality that they were not able to keep the law as they had told God they could.

Paul also points out that the Israelite's hardness of mind persisted for over fifteen hundred years, up to the moment that he wrote this letter. That same veil of pride and self-sufficiency remained over their minds, for each time they heard the law they said, "We can do it." Thus they rejected the truth that Jesus was their Messiah and the only one who could place the law on their hearts and then give them the power by his Holy Spirit to keep it.

Nothing had changed over the thousands of years between the life and times of Moses and of the Jewish community in Corinth, where Paul was currently ministering. Remember, he really understood the heart of the Jewish people because he was one of them. When he wrote from his Roman prison cell to the church in Philippi, which he had founded on his second missionary journey, Paul listed some of his religious masks which stemmed from pride. It was only after he came into a personal relationship with Jesus that he finally saw them for what they were.

> If anyone else thinks he has reasons to put confidence in the flesh, I have more: circumcised on the eighth day, of the people of Israel, of the tribe of

Benjamin, a Hebrew of Hebrews; in regard to the
law, a Pharisee; as for zeal, persecuting the
church; as for legalistic righteousness, faultless.[13]

Today you can stand by the Wailing Wall in Jerusalem and see
many of God's wonderful people still struggling with the same
problem of pride as they read the law out loud, pray and sing the
Psalms, and try their best to keep the traditions and ideals of
Judaism within their own strength.

A synagogue in San Francisco recently printed an advertisement boasting, "We have 613 commandments... If all you've
heard are the top 10, come inside and hear the rest of the story."
Most of us grew up thinking that trying to keep the Ten
Commandments in our own strength was a burden too heavy to
bear. Now this synagogue tells us there are 603 more! When
these dear Jewish people and we Gentiles bow the knee to Jesus
as Messiah and Lord, he takes the commandments off the stones,
places them in our hearts, and provides the power of the Holy
Spirit to live them out in our daily lives. Until we make that
decision, the veil of pride remains. On the other hand, there is
such joy in meeting a Jewish person who has accepted Jesus as
Messiah. They have a spiritual boldness to share their faith that's
wonderful to behold because of all their biblical knowledge,
tradition and culture.

What does the veil represent for us? Here is how Ray Stedman
described the veil:

The veil over Moses' face becomes a symbol of whatever
interferes with and delays the work of the law....The law
has come to kill us, to show us how completely useless it
is for us to try hard to obey God.... But a veil delays that.
It makes us think we really are pleasing God, we are
fulfilling his demands. The veil, therefore, puts off the
death that we need to come to in order to receive the life
that God is willing to give.[14]

Note that Paul is using the current Jewish experience to say to the Christian community in Corinth, "We are _not_ like Moses, right? Don't fall into the same trap that Moses and the Jewish nation have fallen into, trying to live out your Christian life behind the same veils of pride and self-sufficiency."

Unfortunately, the Christian community of our day is not free from being tempted to walk into this same trap, replacing one religious mask for another. We look good on the outside because of a "new mask" we put on for the current situation, but inside we are frightened individuals because we refuse to trust God to make us competent for every new situation.

This tendency is quite prevalent today. I remember our elders interviewing a man for a position in our church. We all enjoyed talking with this delightful man. He answered all our questions with apparent sincerity. After the meeting, one of our elders called one of the man's references. We were informed that this man was a Christian, but he struggled with the problem of promising more than he could deliver. He had in fact not been "sincere" about his skills and gifts. We shared this phone call with him and encouraged him to ask God to help him in that area of pride.

Here is another excerpt from the poem I quoted at the outset:

My surface may seem smooth
But my surface is my mask,
My ever-varying and ever-concealing mask.

Beneath lies no smugness or complacence.
Beneath dwells the real me
In confusion, in fear, in aloneness.

But I hide this. I don't want anybody to know it.
I panic at the thought of my weakness
And my fear being exposed.

That's why I frantically wear a mask to hide behind.
A nonchalant, sophisticated facade,
To help me pretend,
To shield me from the glance that knows.

Many Christians in our communities come out of difficult, perhaps tragic circumstances. Now as followers of Jesus Christ, they still struggle with confusion and fear about God's love for them. It takes time to begin to believe that God really did make a new covenant with us; that he will be our God and we will be his people; and that we can enjoy a loving relationship with him and live out a spiritually fulfilling and meaningful life to his glory and our joy.

Because this new life with Jesus takes time to mature, we find ourselves bringing some of the old thinking patterns and habits from our life before we knew Jesus into our new life with him. Paul encouraged the Roman Christians, "Do not conform any longer to the pattern of this world, but be transformed by the renewing of your mind."[15] Some of those patterns include putting on a veil when we feel inadequate to face a new situation and are too proud to admit that fear to ourselves or others. The veils of pride and hypocrisy come in many forms, all worn out of a need to hide the fading glory of the flesh. Many of us have struggled at one time or another in our Christian life with wearing a veil of self-control over an anxious spirit; a veil of humility over a proud heart; a veil of quietness over our frustration and anger; a veil of defensiveness over our failures; or veils of wealth, skills, and family name over our personal inadequacy. Yet as new-covenant Christians filled with the Holy Spirit, we need to choose to ask ourselves and the Lord: What veils are we wearing today which leave our brothers and sisters thinking we are competent and confident, when in truth we are struggling with incompetence and fear?

I have the privilege of teaching occasionally at a "Higher Power" meeting in a nearby city. This group began when a friend of mine realized that he was surrounded by people who were attending various recovery groups and that in most of those groups, the participants were willing to admit that they needed a higher power than themselves to overcome their particular addictions. My friend and several like-minded men and women decided to offer a meeting patterned after the current recovery groups in his area, with the one difference that the leaders would declare Jesus Christ as their Higher Power. That is a very bold statement in this day and age.

My favorite part of these meetings is when the leader gives people the opportunity to share about their victories or failures of the past week. Each person who desires to share stands up, states his name and addiction. The entire audience responds to that person by name with an attitude of understanding and caring. All the veils are removed and healing is on the way as we pray for them and support them as a spiritual family. Wouldn't it be interesting if we had that same dynamic when we gather together as a church family? Please understand that I am not urging you to discuss all of your personal struggles with a grocery clerk or bank teller in the course of your two-minute   interaction with them. That would be inappropriate. We need to depend on the Holy Spirit for discernment in each circumstance and with each person. The crucial point is to be *willing* to be transparent about our weaknesses, rather than acting hypocritically.

We need to realize that we have the power of the Holy Spirit within us *now* to choose to avoid the trap of Moses, who used to wear a veil when the glory faded; and not to be like the many religious communities who read the law of God and say, "We can do it in our own strength." We can realize and appropriate the secret of living with unveiled faces, which is to turn to the Lord daily in order to have him remove our masks.

Turn to the Lord

But whenever anyone turns to the Lord, the veil is

taken away. Now the Lord is the Spirit, and
where the Spirit of the Lord is, there is freedom.
And we, who with unveiled faces all reflect the
Lord's glory, are being transformed into his likeness with ever-increasing glory, which comes
from the Lord, who is the Spirit.[16]

Paul offers hope to all in the Christian community at Corinth
who no longer desired to be closed and phony, but sought to be
open, transparent, and honest. The good news is, "Whenever
anyone turns to the Lord the veil is taken away." He has already
mentioned that if the Jews turned to Jesus as their Messiah, they
would be set free from the flesh, from pride and self-sufficiency,
from their "we-can-do-it" attitude. He has also reminded them
that when Moses was in the presence of God, he had no need for
the veil.[17] In the same way, when Paul spoke the words of God to
the people, he needed no veil, for he was drawing on the presence and power of God to function as a minister of the new
covenant while teaching and preaching the gospel of Jesus Christ.

The key to transparency is to turn to the Lord, to embrace the
terms of his new covenant. He is our God and we are his people.
He is always present and willing to help us each and every
moment of each day. He is available and powerful enough to
remove the masks we put on but can't take off without him.

We naturally feel that if we allow the Lord to define and
remove our veils, we will be naked, in a no-man's land of vulnera-
bility and weakness. Paul's answer to that is better than we ever
dreamed: "Now the Lord is the Spirit." When Paul says the Lord
is the Spirit, he is not saying that Jesus and the Holy Spirit are
the same person. Rather, he is saying that the Holy Spirit has
been given to us to reveal the character of Christ, and they are
working toward the same purpose. The apostle understood the
ministry of the Holy Spirit after Pentecost as essentially that of
mediating the life, words, and activities of Jesus in and through
his children to a world that needs to hear his good news.

"Where the Lord (Jesus) is, there is freedom." He is not talking about freedom to do whatever we want to do, but freedom to be bold, open, and transparent. There is no need for veils or masks. Christ died and then rose again from the dead to offer us his res- urrection life and power so that we can choose to resist our old lifestyle of self-sufficiency.[18] By his power we can now choose to love and care for people, to speak as Jesus spoke on earth while drawing on the resources of our Heavenly Father. We are free to allow the Holy Spirit to work through us to the glory of Jesus Christ. We are now free from the law and free to be like Jesus.

Peter demonstrated this truth clearly. After he had denied Jesus at his trial, he repented of his sin in the presence of the risen Lord and a few disciples. He was then told to wait in Jerusalem for the coming of the Holy Spirit. Once the Spirit came upon the disciples, Peter was moved to speak out boldly in the courtyard of the temple. Some 3,000 men accepted Jesus as their Messiah based on the word of God, and the power of God in and through a man of God. But it gets even better. A few days after Pentecost, Peter and John were on their way to the temple to pray, when they stopped to heal a lame man. This action drew a crowd, and Peter seized the opportunity to show the Jews from the Old Testament prophets that Jesus was their Messiah. This time he and John were both arrested. While they were in jail overnight, some 5,000 men, having thought through his arguments, reached the conclusion that Jesus was in fact the Messiah.

The next morning, Peter and John were taken before the same Jewish Supreme Court that Jesus had stood before. The religious leaders asked them, "By what power or what name did you do this?" Now here is the secret of new covenant Christianity: "Then Peter, filled with [controlled by] the Holy Spirit, ..." Peter was not drawing on his own strength or some form of self-confidence or pride from the success of the day of Pentecost. He was filled with the indwelling power and confidence that comes from the Holy Spirit, and he said to them, "If we are being called to account today for an act of kindness shown to a cripple and are asked how he was healed, then know this...." Peter told them that they had arrested the wrong men. He turned the tables and put the Supreme Court on trial. "Know this, you and all the people of Israel: it is by the name of Jesus Christ of Nazareth, whom you crucified but whom God raised from the dead, that this man stands before you healed. He is 'the stone you builders rejected, which has become the capstone.'"

Peter went on to preach the gospel of Jesus Christ. Salvation—spiritual healing as symbolized by this physical healing—"'is found in no one else for there is no other name under heaven given to men by which we must be saved.' When they saw the courage of Peter and John and realized that they were unschooled, ordinary men, they were astonished and they took note that these men had been with Jesus."[19] Not only had they been with Jesus during his earthly ministry, but the risen Jesus was within them. He was expressing his resurrection power by the presence of the Holy Spirit living and ministering within these ordinary men. You and I can live a similar kind of life if we will only realize that we must no longer trust in ourselves in any given circumstance, but in God who raises the dead.

Finally, Paul says, "And we, who with unveiled faces all reflect the Lord's glory, are being transformed into his likeness with ever-increasing glory, which comes from the Lord, who is the Spirit." Having turned to the Lord and allowed him to remove our veils of pride, hypocrisy, false humility and so on, we are now in a position, as Moses was, to draw on his power to face our daily lives. We can be unafraid as we live in his strength moment by moment, for we know that the Holy Spirit is quietly transforming us into the character of Jesus Christ. He is able to remove veil after veil. Instead of becoming naked, we find ourselves becoming more and more like Jesus. This transformation is a lifelong process, but the Lord is the one who is behind it. We can rest in his love and timing in order finally and eternally, to become free in him.

Chapter 5

Free at Last!

TO LIVE IN THE LIGHT

Whoever lives by the truth comes into the light, so that it may be seen plainly that what he has done has been done through God.

- Jesus[1]

The Apostle Paul is leading his spiritual family in Corinth out of the darkness of the world system and the old covenant, into the light of the new covenant. Jesus said, "I am the light of the world. Whoever follows me will never walk in darkness, but will have the light of life."[2] He also told his disciples, "You are the light of the world....Let your light shine before men."[3] We live in a spiritually dark world, but once we turn to the Lord and allow him to remove our masks, the light of Jesus in us can penetrate the darkness.

The world around us needs to see and hear of the light of Jesus more than ever before. In the San Francisco Bay area, for example, we have a quarterly New Age magazine called *Common Ground: Resources for Personal Transformation*. Within its pages are hundreds of advertisements for everything from healing and body work, to psychic arts and intuitive sciences, to "lifeworks" and passages. There are also hundreds of workshops, tapes, books and videos which promise to enhance your life. The magazine features articles such as, "Exploring the Mystery of Human Consciousness," "The Healing Path: Illness as an Inner Journey," and "How to Enhance your Intuitive and Creative Abilities."

Whenever I look through a copy of *Common Ground*, I cannot help but think of the spiritual darkness that Paul and his disciples faced as they sought to take the good news of Jesus Christ to the whole known world of their time. The societies around them practiced some 2,000 mystery religions, worshipping countless pagan gods, goddesses and demons. The words in the following advertisement in *Common Ground* would sound very familiar to Paul and the Christians in the early church.

> Gnosis: The Ancient Mystery, Old When Christianity Was Born: This timeless approach to life has been thought extinguished many times. Many efforts have been made to suppress it, especially after the Third Century when Christianity began its all-out effort toward worldly power. Since then gnosis has been present under many names; and even within the structure of the Roman Catholic Church, its deathless essence was recognizable in the life and works of Saint Francis of Assisi, Saint John of the Cross, Meister Eckhart and others. True gnosis cannot be suppressed or eliminated, for it is a knowledge of the heart, independent of books, teachers or traditions. It is free from dogmas and beliefs.[4]

Deceptions like the above would be nothing new to the apostle. Although he lived in a spiritually dark world, Paul was confident in the light that God had given him in Jesus. He now reminds his readers about the darkness of their world and encourages them by explaining the attitude he and his disciples had as they continued to minister among the spiritually blind.

> Therefore, since through God's mercy we have this ministry, we do not lose heart. Rather, we have renounced secret and shameful ways; we do not use deception, nor do we distort the word of God. On the contrary, by setting forth the truth plainly we commend ourselves to every man's conscience in the sight of God. And even if our gospel is veiled, it is veiled to those who are

perishing. The god of this age has blinded the
minds of unbelievers, so that they cannot see the
light of the gospel of the glory of Christ, who is
the image of God.[5]

The apostle reminds us that Christians are recipients of God's
mercy. We have done nothing to deserve it; all we brought into
our new relationship with God was our broken lives. When we
become aware that our new life in Christ is a gift of mercy from
God himself, any temptation to become self-righteous should
quickly fade away. In exchange for our broken, sinful, shameful
lives, God gives us his life. Out of his life the ministry of the new
covenant is able to flow into the spiritual darkness with the message of eternal hope.

Do Not Lose Heart

The result is that "we do not lose heart"—we don't get discouraged and allow circumstances to weigh us down or control us.
We know that behind time and space God is always leading us in
triumph. This spiritual principle of not losing heart in serving
Jesus was beautifully illustrated in the lives of Paul and Silas when
they entered Philippi along with Timothy and Luke on their
second missionary journey. According to Luke's account in Acts,
the foursome did some sightseeing and realized that there was no
synagogue in this Greek-Roman city where they could go to
present the gospel. Jewish custom stated that at least ten families
were necessary in order to form a synagogue. If there were not
enough people, then the smaller group should meet by a local
river for prayer and cleansing rites. Knowing this, Paul and his
disciples went down to the river on the Sabbath to look for other
Jews. Instead, they found a group of Gentile businesswomen.
These women seemed so open to hear Paul's teaching that they
may have been "God-fearers" who had been attracted to the only
living God through some other Jewish teachers.

Led by the Holy Spirit, Paul began to share the good news of
Jesus Christ with them. The Lord opened the heart of a woman

named Lydia, a dealer in purple cloth, along with the members of her household. They all accepted Jesus as their personal Lord and Savior and were immediately baptized. Lydia then invited Paul and his companions to lodge in her home. Their stay in Philippi began on a very encouraging note. Soon, however, the situation took a different turn.

Paul and his friends were returning to the river when they were confronted by a demon-possessed woman who earned a great deal of money for her masters as a fortune-teller. She kept following them for several days and crying out in the streets, "These men are servants of the Most High God, who are telling you the way to be saved." Finally, enough was enough. Paul turned to her and in the name of Jesus Christ cast out the spirit that was living within her. The good news: The girl received back her life and her own mind. The bad news: Her masters became so angry that they hauled Paul and Silas into court. With racist overtones, they falsely accused them of causing a riot because they were "advocating customs unlawful for Romans to accept or practice."[6] The bad news could easily make one "lose heart:" They were stripped, severely flogged, thrown in prison and placed in stocks within the inner cell. Adding insult to injury, this treatment constituted a violation of Paul's civil rights as a Roman citizen.

How would you react if you were placed in the same situation? I have a funny feeling I would be tempted to be discouraged. After all, what kind of reward was this for serving the Lord Jesus and saving a slave girl from a demonic lifestyle? Well, according to Luke's telling of this story, Paul and Silas sat in prison that night praying and singing hymns to God. The other prisoners were listening to them. Remember, this new covenant ministry is never boring. Suddenly the city experienced a major earthquake which caused all the prison gates to swing open and the chains to fall off the prisoners. The jailer woke up with the thought that all his prisoners had escaped and decided that it was better to kill himself than face the wrath of Rome. The apostle stopped him with the words, "We are all here." The jailer, overwhelmed by the circumstances, rushed into Paul and Silas' cell and in a trembling voice asked, "Sirs, what must I do to be saved?" Without blinking an eye in the bright light of the torches, Paul responded, "Believe in the Lord Jesus Christ and you will be saved—you and your household."

Paul and Silas went on to explain the good news, and all the members of the jailer's family also invited Jesus to become their Lord and Savior. They became "new creatures" in Christ, changed from within. The whole group was then baptized in the middle of the night. The next day, the Roman judge released Paul and Silas, but not without apologizing for violating their civil rights. The foursome then visited Lydia one last time and continued on their missionary journey to the southern port city of Thessalonica.

Paul and his companions did not lose heart because they knew that God, who is invisible but always present, would lead them and strengthen them. They had personally experienced the joy of seeing God use their difficult circumstances to bring about the salvation of two entire families. This is the kind of excitement all of us can experience when we choose to live in the spiritual world and the natural world at the same time.

Nothing Secret

Paul goes on to explain why he and his brothers and sisters did not give in to the temptation to be discouraged on this occasion. He says, "We have renounced secret and shameful ways." He may be referring to the sexual immorality that was occurring among the new believers based on teaching from some of their false prophets. These teachers advocated immediate gratification of all physical needs, whether food, shelter, clothing—or sex. Paul had challenged their teaching in his earlier letter to the Corinthians:

> "Everything is permissible for me"—but not
> everything is beneficial. "Everything is permissi-
> ble for me"—but I will not be mastered by

anything. "Food for the stomach and the stomach for food"—but God will destroy them both. The body is not meant for sexual immorality, but for the Lord, and the Lord for the body.... Flee from sexual immorality. All other sins a man commits are outside his body, but he who sins sexually sins against his own body. Do you not know that your body is a temple of the Holy Spirit, who is in you, whom you have received from God? You are not your own, you were bought at a price. Therefore, honor God with your body.[7]

Paul assures the Corinthian church that he and his disciples avoid such compromising behavior. He reminds his readers that he is being up-front with them about God's truth, and is in no way trying to deceive them. Remember, he had already told his spiritual family, "Unlike so many, we do not peddle the word of God for profit. On the contrary, in Christ we speak before God with sincerity, like men sent from God."[8] His life and message were an open book and he was going to trust in the Spirit and the Word of God to change people's hearts, rather than resort to some man-made philosophy for success.

Human philosophies, including well-meaning, morally attractive value systems, are still being used in our day to get people's attention. For instance, a certain church which claims to be Christian ran expensive advertisements in national magazines giving their history, freely using the name of Jesus, and inviting all the readers to join their church. They claim: They have a low divorce rate; they don't drink, smoke, or use drugs; they are moral, upright, clean living; they love to sing, dance and play games; they are good givers to worthy causes; they are high achievers in sports, politics and entertainment; they have low cancer and heart disease rates; their membership has doubled in the last 10 years; they are against drugs, homosexuality, abortion and immorality; their goal is peace. Yet, behind this slick advertisement lie a variety of theological traps, two of the more serious being their refusal to recognize the deity of Jesus Christ, and their insistence that salvation is earned by works.

Christians, however, do not need to resort to gimmicks to proclaim Christ. In the "Higher Power" meetings I mentioned earlier, the leaders decided to declare publicly that Jesus is the "Higher Power" who loves people and can help them deal with their pain and failure. This intent was openly stated, nothing hidden. The meetings I have attended have been filled with some 200 men, women and children who are looking for spiritual help. The leadership team includes several ex-convicts and reformed drug addicts, and a former prostitute. One leader was a victim of incest, but is now healed and openly tells others about the love of Jesus. The key, though, is that these spiritual changes in the lives of the leadership have been the best advertisement anyone would need of the truth that Jesus can make a difference in a person's life. "Higher Power" continues to grow and is meeting a real need in a suffering community.

No Distortions

Another reason Paul did not become discouraged in his ministry was because he did not "distort the word of God." He did not water down the word of God or change it to fit certain needs, as the false teachers apparently were doing. They taught that salvation was earned by works;[9] that marriage to unbelievers was permissible;[10] and that sexual immorality was not sinful. In our own day we see people who say they believe in Jesus as the Christ, yet they also say that Christians should be both healthy and wealthy. This false philosophy is failing quickly because those Christians are now getting sick and going broke like the rest of us. This has nothing to do with a lack of faith, but everything to do with the basic spiritual principle we started with: that all these physical, emotional and spiritual trials are allowed in our lives so that we will no longer trust in ourselves but in God who raises the dead. Paul again wants to drive home the important spiritual principle that he is finally free *not* to distort the Word of God. He was confident that God would be responsible for how it would be received and how it would flourish.

Several years ago I had an experience that I will never forget. I was invited to lunch by a businessman who was helping me in our ministry to single adults. He was a married man with several young children. When I walked into the restaurant, I noticed that he had invited a young divorced mother to join us for lunch. I recognized her from several of our meetings so I was not surprised to see her. I assumed that she must have run into some personal problems; presumably my "co-worker" was trying to help her, and he was going to include me in the process. Within a few moments of placing our order, my friend asked me a question which I thought was very strange: "Ron, what do you think of a loving, caring relationship?" and then looked towards the woman. I asked him what he meant by those terms and he told me that he found himself having a "loving, caring relationship" with this young divorced woman and that their relationship was developing. The hair on the back of my neck stood up and I saw flashing warning lights. I asked abruptly, "You mean as a married man with several children you are planning on or are already committing adultery with this woman?" He quickly replied that I was being crude. I said, "Well, let me be real crude in order to make it clear to both of you...."

I won't repeat what I said at that point except to tell you that he interrupted me and said angrily, "I don't have to sit here and listen to you speak to us in that manner." "No, you don't," I said as I stood up and left with a broken heart over the blindness of my friend, the distortion of God's Word and the corruption within this relationship. This couple broke up a short time later; he was removed from leadership at the church; his wife divorced him and the children were devastated for years. I later heard that he and his ex-wife each remarried other Christians and are now back in fellowship with Jesus Christ. They have also apparently reconciled with their families, but not without some painful consequences. "We do not use deception, nor do we distort the word of God" by calling adultery a loving, caring relationship.

Tell It Like It Is

In contrast to the false teachers, Paul drew on the power of the Spirit to function as a minister of the new covenant by "setting forth the truth plainly." That means simply telling people what God has said, without trying to defend it or change it so it won't offend people.

Recently a young couple who were looking forward to being married asked me to perform their wedding ceremony. After some basic questions as to the date, location, and other logistics, I asked them, "Are you presently involved in a sexual relationship?" They answered, "Yes." I said I appreciated their honesty, and asked them to read another passage by the apostle Paul on the same subject, which says in part, "It is God's will that you be sanctified; that you should avoid sexual immorality."[11] I then went on to explain God's definition of "sexual immorality," which is any sexual activity outside of a marriage relationship. Since they were not married, I asked them if they were willing to stop their sexual relationship until their wedding day. They said they would get back to me. Two weeks later they called to say that they wanted to begin their new married life with God's blessing, and by his power they would stop having a sexual relationship until their wedding day. Their family members thought that they were crazy and that I was worse than that. I recently had the privilege of marrying this couple. On their wedding day they told me that they had remained sexually pure from the time they gave the Lord and me their word of honor.

Trust God for the Results

Not only is Paul willing to set forth the truth plainly, but he also "commends himself to every man's conscience." He and his disciples made an appeal to the mind. They were not forced to invent a message from God that played on the emotions and by-passed the intellect. The conscience is the process of thought which helps man distinguish between what is morally good and morally bad, based on God's definition of good and bad. While our conscience has been damaged by sin, it has sufficient discernment to know truth when it hears it, even if it rejects that truth. In this case, Paul is showing men and women everywhere that Jesus is the risen Son of God and the only one who can produce in them the godly life they want to live, but are unable to in their own strength. We all have a sense of God's righteous demands and our own failed attempts to measure up. As Paul wrote to the Roman Christians:

> The wrath of God is being revealed from heaven against all the godlessness and wickedness of men who suppress the truth by their wickedness, since what may be known about God is plain to them, because God has made it plain to them. For since the creation of the world God's invisible qualities, his eternal power and divine nature have been clearly seen, being understood from what has been made, so that men are without excuse. For although they knew God they neither glorified him as God nor gave thanks to him, but their thinking became futile and their foolish hearts were darkened.[12]

Paul also ministered "in the sight of God." Once again, he refers to his awareness of the presence and power of God. The apostle's life, motives, and actions were transparent before the Lord. He sensed his daily accountability to God for his ministry. He and his disciples lived out the truth in the sight of God (and the Corinthians). In the end, Paul was free from a ministry of manipulation in which he was the only one who could produce the results. Rather, he simply trusted God for the spiritual results of their teaching and preaching. This spiritual principle was clearly taught by our Lord Jesus when he told his disciples. "This is what the kingdom of God is like. A man scatters seed on the ground. Night and day, whether he sleeps or gets up, the seed sprouts and grows, though he does not know how. All by itself the soil produces grain—first the stalk, then the head, then the full kernel in the head. As soon as the grain is ripe, he puts the sickle to it, because the harvest has come."[13]

Some Won't See

Next Paul turns his focus to the non-Christian community, which included some of the Jews as well as the false teachers he had to contend with in Corinth. First he gives his spiritual children the bad news: "Even if our gospel is veiled, it is veiled to those who are perishing. The god of this age has blinded the minds of unbelievers, so that they cannot see the light of the gospel of the glory of Christ, who is the image of God." As Paul preached the good news that Jesus Christ was and is the Son of God, he realized (as he stated earlier[14]) that his message was being heard by two groups, those who were in the process of perishing and those who were being saved. He knew that pride and self-sufficiency were veils over the minds and hearts of those who were perishing.

The "god of this world," Satan, had blinded the minds of some of the Jews so that they could no longer see the truth. The Jews believed that salvation came by doing good works. The truth that came in Jesus was that man can be saved by the grace of God if he confesses Jesus as the risen Son of God and the Messiah. This message was not good news to a spiritually blinded Jew because he believed that Jesus was a blasphemer and a deceiver who could never qualify to be Messiah. The Greeks, on the other hand, were being blinded by Satan so that they came to believe that there were many gods or many ways to a supreme god.

Jesus as Lord

The way Paul and his disciples were able to prevail against the opposition of the false teachers was to be ministers of the truth; that is, to teach and live out the truth of God as revealed in the Scriptures. They had only one message:

> For we do not preach ourselves but Jesus Christ as Lord, and ourselves as your servants for Jesus' sake. For God, who said, "Let light shine out of darkness," made his light shine in our hearts to give us the light of the knowledge of the glory of God in the face of Christ.[15]

This represents the good news for unbelievers! In spite of their resistance, the veils they wore, and the work of Satan who sought to distort the person of Christ, Paul was saying that he and his disciples continued to preach Jesus Christ as Lord. Jesus was not merely a prophet, a teacher, or a moral man. He was and is the long-promised Messiah of whom the prophets spoke, the one who came to suffer and die for the sins of humanity[16] and then was raised again by the power of his Heavenly Father.[17] He now rules over heaven and earth as King of Kings and Lord of Lords.[18]

The good news is that Jesus can break through all spiritual, intellectual and emotional opposition and penetrate any darkness within the mind and heart of man. The God who commanded the light to shine out of darkness at the beginning of creation is the same one who has shone in our hearts, and so we are empowered to carry that light of truth into our spiritually darkened world. There is hope for unbelievers. No matter how proud and stubborn they are, no matter how many masks they wear, the God who said, "Let there be light," can open the eyes of any spiritually blind person directly or through his servants and his Word.

Suddenly a Bright Light

No one knew this truth better than Paul, who, some five years after he wrote this letter, would stand before the Jewish people as a prisoner of Rome and tell them of his spiritual conversion thirty years earlier:

> I persecuted the followers of this Way to their death, arresting both men and women and throwing them into prison, as also the high priest and all the Council can testify. I even obtained letters from them to their brothers in Damascus, and went there to bring these people as prisoners to Jerusalem to be punished.

> About noon as I came near Damascus, suddenly a bright light from heaven flashed around me. I fell to the ground and heard a voice say to me, "Saul! Saul! Why do you persecute me?" "Who are you, Lord?" I asked. "I am Jesus of Nazareth, whom you are persecuting," he replied.[19]

The light of Jesus Christ penetrated the deep spiritual darkness that Paul (then Saul) was living in and liberated him to become a minister of the new covenant. Later Paul would give that same testimony to King Agrippa. He proclaimed that the Lord Jesus had told him that he was to be sent to the Jews and the Gentiles "to open their eyes and turn them from darkness to light and from the power of Satan to God."[20]

In his ministry, Paul was free to depend on the power of Jesus to penetrate the veils which Satan had placed over the minds of the Jews and Gentiles with the light of his good news of salvation. As Chuck Colson has so aptly described the process:

> New life in the Spirit is conceived in the secret place of

the soul, hidden from human eyes. This is the wonder and mystery of God's regeneration of men and women. And never in this life will we quite know how God calls his people to himself.

What we do know is that the wind of the Spirit blows where he wills. We hear the sound, we see the evidences, but we know not how this mysterious breath of God touches human hearts. God builds his church in the most unlikely ways and places, stirring the convictions of the heart, bringing men and women to the knowledge of sin, to repentance, to the Savior himself—and knotting them together in his body.[21]

The apostle Paul and his disciples were free to take the light of Christ into a very dark world. They were spiritually empowered to speak the truth of the gospel of Jesus Christ plainly and simply. It did not matter if the audience were men and women in the process of becoming believers or in the process of perishing—they were going to live out their lives in the sight of God and teach the truth to anyone who would listen. They hoped with their whole heart that everyone, including the false teachers and spiritually blinded Jews and Greeks, would respond to the truth of God as revealed in the life of his risen Son, Jesus.

Chapter 6

Free~at Last!
TO DEAL WITH WEAKNESS

He knows the way that I take; when he has tested me, I will come forth as gold.

- Job[1]

In August 1977, my wife and our two young sons traveled a few days ahead of me to the beautiful Swiss village of Villar, where we planned to spend a month relaxing together as a family. As I rode the train from Zurich, I reflected on a good but highly intense year of work. Suddenly, I realized that I had been living under tremendous stress. As the train pulled into the station, I felt a weight of exhaustion far heavier than just the fatigue of travel and jet lag. I finally arrived at our chalet, where my family greeted me with birthday presents and a special dinner.

Our vacation could not have started out any better. We went hiking in the mountains and ice skating at the local outdoor rink. We delighted in meeting people and enjoying family time together. Each day seemed to hold wonderful new adventures.

One morning about mid-way through our vacation, I went down to a small outdoor restaurant which boasted a panoramic view of the Swiss Alps. My table overlooked the rolling hills of summer wildflowers, and I could hear the music of the cowbells as the herds wandered up and down the mountain pastures. When the waiter brought my breakfast, I reached for my cup of coffee. Just as I was about to taste it, I dropped the cup on the table, spilling coffee over my rolls and butter. The waiter quickly cleaned up the mess and brought me another order. I thanked him and picked up the fresh cup of coffee. Once again, the cup dropped out of my hand. Something was wrong, seriously wrong. At first I thought I was drinking too much caffeine and needed to cut back. Would that life's problems could be so quickly analyzed! In fact, the cause of my new physical problems would be revealed to me in stages over the next several months.

Soon after we returned home, I began having difficulty focusing my eyes. I had to wear dark sunglasses because my eyes became oversensitive to light. I went to a doctor, who diagnosed me as a "borderline diabetic" and put me on a special diet. I maintained his diet, but things just got worse. I was rapidly losing weight. I had to tape my eyes to keep them closed at night, and I noticed that they were starting to bulge out of their sockets. I could feel emotional stress and quiet panic building in my heart and was tempted to give in. At times I lost self-control and broke out in bursts of anger, which stunned those around me as well as myself. Fortunately, my wife, family and friends were praying for me as I sought the Lord's peace and strength to cope with this physical and emotional affliction.

God gave me his peace and strength, and in time I realized how faithful he was to answer my prayers. One evening at one of our church services, an older woman took one look at me and said, "Ron, you don't look well. Are you OK?" I told her that I wasn't feeling well, but my doctor had said it was because I was a borderline diabetic. She quickly refuted that opinion, saying, "I have seen those kind of eyes before and I think that you need to see another doctor. It looks like you are developing a goiter on your neck which could mean that your thyroid gland is enlarged." She added that this could be what was affecting my eyes, which were continuing to be pushed out of their sockets.

The next day, I went to the local clinic. Additional blood tests showed that I had a seriously damaged thyroid. This condition had caused me to contract Grave's Disease, which was affecting my eyes. I would not wish the struggles I experienced over the next two years on my worst enemy. I became physically weak, emotionally distressed and spiritually confused. I finally had my thyroid removed, underwent radiation treatments, and had surgery to correct my eyes and tighten my eye lids. At times I was emotionally devastated, but I thank God that I was able to experience the presence and peace of the Lord in my heart and mind, which in turn enabled me to trust him through this ordeal. My eyes have now fully recovered except for a slight aversion to bright lights, and thyroid medication has helped stabilized my metabolism.

The lessons I learned during that difficult period still hold true. The only way I can keep from being completely crushed in the storms of this life is to rely on God and not on myself. This is the same lesson that Paul learned through one of his trials in Asia. He described it as follows: "Indeed, in our hearts we felt the sentence of death. But this happened that we might not rely on ourselves but on God, who raises the dead."[2]

Having learned to trust Jesus in the midst of so many of life's storms, Paul encouraged his disciples in Corinth to also turn to God for the freedom to cope with the various afflictions and crippling blows of life. He was speaking from a wealth of experience:

> Three times I was beaten with rods, once I was stoned, three times I was shipwrecked, I spent a night and a day in the open sea, I have been constantly on the move. I have been in danger from rivers, in danger from bandits, in danger from my own countrymen, in danger from Gentiles; in danger in the city, in danger in the country, in

danger at sea.... I have labored and toiled and
have often gone without sleep; I have known
hunger and thirst and have often gone without
food.... Besides everything else, I face daily the
pressure of my concern for all the churches.[3]

Jars of Clay

Just as Paul listened to his contemporaries, he would listen to
our stories of our stressful lives. If he were alive today, we can be
assured that he would faithfully point out to us from his own
experiences of failure that he really understands us. He would
also remind us to go back to the basics: to understand that God is
using the difficult times in our lives to bring us closer to Jesus. In
this process, Jesus wants to live within us and have the freedom
to express himself through us to a dark and struggling humanity
that needs to see the light of the love of God. Here's how Paul
explained it to the Corinthians:

But we have this treasure in jars of clay to show
that this all-surpassing power is from God and
not from us. We are hard pressed on every side,
but not crushed; perplexed, but not in despair;
persecuted, but not abandoned; struck down, but
not destroyed. We always carry around in our
body the death of Jesus, so that the life of Jesus
may also be revealed in our body. For we who are
alive are always being given over to death for
Jesus' sake, so that his life may be revealed in our
mortal body. So then, death is at work in us, but
life is at work in you.[4]

The "treasure" Paul refers to is "the light of the knowledge of
the glory of God in the face of Christ." Once the spiritual lights
were turned on in his darkened heart, Paul finally understood
that the man he thought was a blasphemer and a political rebel
actually was the Christ, the Son of the living God.

The "treasure" is the truth that Jesus is the Lord and his word of grace is salvation to all who place their faith in him.

Eugene Peterson provides helpful insight into this treasure in his Scripture paraphrase, *The Message.*

[Some people] are stone-blind to the dayspring brightness of the Message that shines with Christ, who gives us the best picture of God we'll ever get.

Remember, our Message is not about ourselves; we're proclaiming Jesus Christ, the Master. All we are is messengers, errand runners from Jesus for you. It started when God said, "Light up the darkness!" and our lives filled up with light as we saw and understood God in the face of Christ, all bright and beautiful.

If you only look at us, you might well miss the brightness. We carry this precious Message around in the unadorned clay pots of our ordinary lives. That's to prevent anyone from confusing God's incomparable power with us."[5]

Christians have this treasure, Paul says, "in jars of clay." A jar is designed to contain something. In the case of a Christian, we are designed by God himself to contain his risen Son Jesus. Paul reminded the Ephesian Christians that Christ dwells or makes his home in our hearts. He reminded the Galatian Christians: "I have been crucified with Christ and I no longer live, but Christ lives in me. The life I live in the body, I live by faith in the Son of God, who loved me and gave himself for me."[6]

Note again that *we* are not the treasure, just the containers for the treasure. Paul tells the Corinthians that he is a human being made of flesh and blood, just like they are. He draws a metaphor from the pottery shops in the Corinthian marketplace, describing our physical bodies as nothing more than clay pots. The truth of this metaphor is based on the Genesis account of man's origin: "The Lord God formed the man from the *dust* of the ground and breathed into his nostrils the breath of life, and the man became a living being."[7]

Although man was designed as a clay jar to contain the living God, who in turn makes man's life purposeful, useful and fulfilling, most people in the world unfortunately live futile, lonely, and despairing lives. We can see it all around us. In order to hold back the pain, they turn to relationships that prove to be destructive, jobs that eventually are meaningless, drugs of all sorts—and many resort to the ultimate trip of suicide.

This despair and emptiness can affect followers of Jesus Christ as well. It can happen whenever we continue to put our confidence in our personality, our strength, our position, our wealth, … our flesh. Paul certainly understood the problem we all have when we first come into a personal relationship with Jesus as our Lord. In a real sense we want Jesus to be Lord of our lives, but we want to remain in control, too. We struggle with choosing the *source* of our strength when seeking to cope with our present difficulties. Should we depend on our own strength or on Jesus, who now lives in us and has given us his Holy Spirit to empower us daily?

As we saw earlier, Paul demonstrated this struggle of working out his new life as a Christian when he wrote to the Philippian Christian community.

> If anyone else thinks he has reasons to put confidence in the flesh, I have more: circumcised on the eighth day, of the people of Israel, of the tribe of Benjamin, a Hebrew of the Hebrews; in regard to the law [of Moses], a Pharisee; as for zeal, persecuting the church; as for legalistic righteousness, faultless.[8]

In other words, if we looked at Paul's life before he accepted Jesus as his Messiah, we would see that he came from a wonderful family who lived according to the letter of the law of Moses. As commanded in Leviticus, Paul's parents took him to the priest to be circumcised when he was eight days old, so that he would inherit the blessings of God's covenant with Abraham. Paul came from pure Jewish stock dating back to Abraham, Isaac and Jacob. He was a true "blue blood" of Israel. The tribe of Benjamin was Israel's elite, a tribe of honor among the twelve. He was a Hebrew of the Hebrews, the model of the purest of the pure. His father was a Pharisee, one who separated himself from the influence of this world and had a high regard for the Law of God, the Torah. Paul was such a true Jew that he was willing to persecute any individual or group who did not agree with the theology of the Pharisees. He believed in his heart that according to the law of Moses, he would be found blameless in the sight of God.

You could not have a better set of religious credentials in Paul's day and age. Opportunity, reward, position, and power were at his fingertips. Why would he need to rely on God daily with that kind of pure religious background, the ideal parents, the preeminent tribe, the ultimate calling, and the perfectly blameless life? This was the quintessential success story of a young man living in his society, the same "crème de la crème" as a person leaving the halls of Stanford or Harvard with an advanced degree, backed by a well-known and successful family.

In light of his new relationship with Jesus Christ, whom he personally met on the Road to Damascus, Paul looked back on his life before Christ and said:

> But whatever was to my profit I now consider loss for the sake of Christ. What is more, I consider everything a loss compared to the surpassing greatness of knowing Christ Jesus my Lord, for whose sake I have lost all things. I consider

them rubbish, that I may gain Christ and be found in him, not having a righteousness of my own that comes from the law, but that which is through faith in Christ—the righteousness that comes from God and is by faith.[9]

The reason the treasure is contained in jars of clay, Paul says, is "to show that this all-surpassing power is from God and not from us." This is the same power that caused light to shine out of darkness at creation, the same power that can break through hardened hearts and minds and convert enemies of our Lord into servants of Jesus Christ. That presence and power is expressed in and through man by means of the Holy Spirit, to show that the source of that power is God, not man. That has been God's way of working through the ages as he has demonstrated his plan of salvation in the world, using weak men and women to fulfill his purposes.

Let's now examine a few of the clay jars that God has used over the centuries. These examples will assure us that God doesn't want us to be super-heroes, just servants who will trust in *his* strength.

Abraham and Sarah: Parents of the Nation of Israel

Abraham and Sarah were long past the age of child-bearing when God chose them to begin the new nation which he was forming. God had approached Abraham when he was about 75 years old and told him that he and his barren wife Sarah would have a child, who would father a race of people from whom the Messiah would come. It is one thing to have God promise this older couple that they would have a child, but it is another thing for them to trust God for the next 25 years and still be barren. When Abraham was 99 years old, the Lord appeared to him again and told him that he would become "the father of a multitude of nations"—yet Sarah remained childless at 89. Finally the Lord told Abraham that they would have a baby the following year.

When Sarah heard the news of this plan, she—

> laughed to herself as she thought, "After I am
> worn out and my master is old, will I now have
> this pleasure?" Then the Lord said to Abraham,
> "Why did Sarah laugh and say, 'Will I really have
> a child, now that I am old?' Is anything too hard
> for the Lord? I will return to you at the appoint-
> ed time next year and Sarah will have a son."[10]

The following year, Sarah, an aged clay jar, gave birth to Isaac
(which means laughter). He was the child of promise and the
firstborn of the nation of Israel.

Moses: Shepherd of the Nation of Israel

Generations later, the Jewish nation was in slavery in Egypt.
The Pharaoh realized that the Jewish slave population was
increasing and would soon outnumber the Egyptian people, so
he established a policy to have all Hebrew male babies killed by
the Egyptian mid-wives. When this policy failed, he ordered that
all Hebrew baby boys be thrown into the Nile river. When
Moses was born, his Hebrew mother refused to drown him, so
she placed him in a small papyrus basket and hid him in the reeds
by the river bank. The Pharaoh's daughter found him there and
sent for a wet nurse, who just happened to be Moses's mother.
Thus, the young Hebrew boy began his life in the palace of the
Egyptian King.

One day, at the age of forty, Moses decided to visit his fellow
Israelites who were suffering in slavery under Pharaoh. Upon
walking into a situation where an Egyptian was beating a
Hebrew, Moses killed the Egyptian and buried the body in the
sand. "Moses thought that his own people would realize that
God was using him to rescue them, but they did not."[11] So he
fled to Midian and lived there as a foreigner. He had acquired
the knowledge that God had called him to become the deliverer

of his people, but instead of waiting on God, Moses took matters into his own hands. As a result, he became a murderer and lived as an outcast for some forty years. But God used this situation as part of his divine plan to prepare Moses to become the deliverer of his people, not as a man of power and authority, but as a humble shepherd fully dependent on him.

While tending his flocks one day, Moses saw a burning bush that failed to be consumed by its own fire. Upon investigation, he heard a voice saying,

> "I am the God of your father, the God of Abraham, the God of Isaac and the God of Jacob….Now the cry of the Israelites has reached me, and I have seen the way the Egyptians are oppressing them. So now, go. I am sending you to Pharaoh to bring my people the Israelites out of Egypt."
>
> But Moses said to God, "Who am I, that I should go to Pharaoh and bring the Israelites out of Egypt?" And God said, "I will be with you."[12]

This once proud and powerful leader was now standing before God as a broken man with no influence or self-confidence. God was asking Moses to go *with* him in a position of weakness so that the Egyptians could see the power and glory of God in him. God was saying, "Don't count on yourself, Moses. Count on me to work through you. You make the choice to show up, and I'll provide the power and do the delivering."

Moses became fearful that the Israelites in Egypt would not accept him or his message based on his history with them as a murderer, refugee, and now a shepherd who had been away for some forty years. He knew that if he went to the people and told them about his experience of meeting "God," they would ask him, "Oh yeah? What is his name?" So God told Moses, "I am who I am. This is what you are to say to the Israelites: 'I am has sent me to you.'"[13]

God has many names, but this name "Yahweh" means I am—present tense. He is the eternally self-existent one. In this context, God is telling Moses that HE IS whatever Moses needs him to be. "Moses, I am your power, I am your courage, I am your wisdom, I am your knowledge. Moses, I am everything you need when you go down to Egypt—not only to face your brothers, but also to encounter the Egyptian king, his army, as well as his wise men and magicians." God showed Moses three miraculous signs that he would be able to use in case the people doubted that it was truly God who had sent him.

Then Moses raised another objection: "O Lord, I have never been eloquent, neither in the past nor since you have spoken to your servant. I am slow of speech and tongue."[14] He was stating exactly what God already knew—that in his own natural strength, he was not adequate for the job. God had to remind Moses again that he was aware of his limitations. God replied, "Who gave man his mouth? Who makes him deaf or mute? Who gives him sight or makes him blind? Is it not I, the Lord? Now go; I will help you speak and will teach you what to say."[15] In other words, Moses' impediment was irrelevant!

Finally, Moses asked God to send someone else. At this point, the Lord got angry with Moses—not because he was weak, fearful, or inept at public speaking, but because he would not trust God to use him. Even here, though, God was gracious and told Moses that he would provide a partner, Moses' brother Aaron, who was a good speaker. God promised to help both of them speak and to teach them what to do. In time, Pharaoh let the Israelites leave Egypt and go into the Promised Land.

Moses had the treasure of God's life in his fragile clay jar. When God called Moses to work in his name, he was not depending on Moses' ability, confidence, power or influence. Rather, as he told him at the burning bush, "I am all the confidence, power, influence, wisdom and ability that you will ever need to accomplish the task I have placed before you. Therefore, place your faith in me and show up in Egypt as a humble Hebrew shepherd. I will empower you in such a way that not only will my people be free at last after 400 years of slavery, but the Egyptian king and all his people will see that the all-surpassing power is from me and not from you."

Gideon: Mighty Warrior for Israel

After Moses died and Joshua led the Israelites into the Promised Land, the people soon rebelled against God. They forsook the Lord, served the Baals (the false gods of the local people), and intermarried with the Canaanites in hopes of creating military alliances. As a result of their disobedience, God allowed their Midianite enemies to rule over them for some seven years, and the people of Israel were forced to live in caves like animals. Each year at harvest time, they would look out on their hard-worked fields and helplessly watch the Midianites (who were traveling traders), Amalekites (who were god-defying), and other eastern peoples come and usurp their crops and livestock. These invaders:

> camped on the land and ruined the crops all the
> way to Gaza and did not spare a living thing for
> Israel, neither sheep nor cattle nor donkeys. They
> came up with their livestock and their tents like
> swarms of locusts. It was impossible to count the
> men and their camels; they invaded the land to
> ravage it. Midian so impoverished the Israelites
> that they cried out to the Lord for help.[16]

In response, God sent a prophet to remind the people that this condition was a direct result of their own disobedience to him. Nevertheless, he then appeared to Gideon (another "clay jar"), who was threshing wheat in a wine press to hide it from the Midianites. The angel of the Lord addressed him as a "mighty warrior," which Gideon was quick to point out was not true! He asked the angel why the Israelites were in bondage again, if it were true that the Lord was with them. The angel tested Gideon and said, "Go in the strength you have, and save Israel out of Midian's hand. Am I not sending you?"[17]

Gideon then "pulled a Moses" by saying in effect, "Listen, angel, I know who I am. I am the least of the least and I am the youngest in my family. I have no courage, influence or authority." But God promised him, "I will be with you, and you will strike down all the Midianites together."[18]

After the Lord assured him with several miraculous signs, Gideon moved out toward the camp of the 135,000 Midianites with his army of some 32,000, only to discover that the Lord thought he had too many men. God did not want the Israelites to think that they had defeated the enemy in their own strength, so he told Gideon to send 22,000 fearful men home. This was still too many men for the Lord, so he gave him another test and whittled the troops down to 300—impossible odds against an army of 135,000.

At this point, Gideon had to *choose* to believe that God would provide the power and courage for this battle. God encouraged him once again by allowing him to overhear a Midianite telling his cohorts about a dream in which he saw the sword of Gideon defeating their army. Once he believed that God would give him the victory, Gideon bowed and worshiped the Lord, then returned to his camp to rouse his men: "Get up! The Lord has given the Midianite camp into your hands!"[19] He divided his men into three groups of 100 and placed them on the mountain tops surrounding the Midianite camp in the valley below. He had his men light candles and place them inside clay pots. When the signal was given, they blew trumpets, broke the clay pots and shouted, "For the Lord and for Gideon!" This act of faith by Gideon and his 300 men so confused the enemies of Israel that they rose up out of their sleep and 120,000 of them managed to kill each other in the darkness. They chased the final 15,000 men and their two kings and killed them. Finally, Israel's seven-year bondage was over because one fearful but faithful man was willing to trust God for victory.

When Paul wrote about how God created all of us as *clay jars* designed to contain him so that he could express himself through us, his readers undoubtedly thought back to some of the above-mentioned Old Testament saints. He knew that though the names change in every generation, the spiritual principle continues. He was also discovering that the same truths were being applied to his own life and should be applied to the lives of all Christians in every generation. They all boil down to the lesson Paul learned in his trial in Asia, which happened so that he would "not rely on [himself] but on God, who raises the dead."[20]

Paul continues, explaining to the Corinthians that living in a fallen world is very difficult. However, we are to remember that God is with us and in us and will provide the power necessary to live each day if we just ask him.

Stress, Stress, Stress...

Paul uses four illustrations from his own experiences that have spiritual relevance in our own lives today. Keep in mind that all human beings are fragile clay jars and that Christians and non-Christians alike experience difficult circumstances. The key for Christians is the truth that the Lord Jesus lives within them and has filled them with his Holy Spirit to provide the power, wisdom, courage, love or whatever else they need to deal with the immediate cause of their stress. God then uses this attitude of total reliance on him to draw non-Christians and weak Christians to himself as they see him living within us.

"We are hard pressed on every side, but not crushed." The term translated *hard pressed*, or *afflicted*, denotes pressure from outside ourselves. Paul draws this figure of being crushed from Roman culture. When a suspected criminal was arrested, he was taken to a special room for questioning. If the authorities thought he was not telling them the truth, they would pin the suspect to the floor and have two slaves lay a heavy marble slab on his chest. They would ask for the information again, and if they thought that he was still lying, they would order another heavy slab. This would continue until the prisoner either confessed or was crushed to death.

Paul uses this illustration to talk about the afflictions, pressures, and stressful circumstances he and his disciples faced on both a physical and emotional level. As we have seen, Paul, Timothy, Titus, Silas and others were clay jars who experienced all kinds of troubles in their ministry.

The difference between the Christian and the non-Christian facing the same kind of trial, is that strength is available to the believer from within to resist the external pressure that threatens to crush us. That power is Christ himself. If Christians choose to rely on that resource, they will not be *crushed* by their current stress. One of my dear friends has been quite successfully self-employed in commercial real estate. He has a reputation as a man who loves the Lord and is very generous with his time, money, and other possessions. He dedicates time to helping the poor, opens his home for Bible teachers to share the gospel with his neighbors and friends, and has served as an elder in his church. He owns a vacation home in a resort area and has reserved blocks of time for pastors and other Christian leaders to stay there, relax with their families and be refreshed. His wife reaches out to the widows and senior citizens in the community. As a couple, they are known for their gracious love and hospitality.

Over the last two years, his business has taken a hit as the market has collapsed from under him and thousands of others in the same field. At about the same time, he and his investment partners were sued over a piece of property, and lost. In order to settle his part of the judgment, he has been forced to sell his home and some of his other assets, rent out his vacation home, and cut back on his ability to be financially generous. We frequently meet for lunch, and I ask him how he is handling all this stress. He answers that he is doing well, "in the things that are important to God." He knows that Christ is his strength. Even if he were to lose all of his assets, he affirms, he would still be the same person who loves Jesus. He and his wife would still seek to be generous and show hospitality in whatever way they could.

During one of our recent lunch conversations, I asked him if this were a painful experience. Yes, he said. But he added that in this stressful season he had drawn closer to the Lord and wouldn't trade that experience for anything he had lost in the process. Did he feel crushed? No, in fact, he felt stronger spiritually. The pressure has not subsided, but he and his wife continue to serve the Lord faithfully in the midst of it. Though they feel *hard pressed*, Jesus Christ lives within them, countering the pressure from without and protecting them from the fear of being *crushed* by the heavy circumstances of life.

Next, the apostle says, "[we are] perplexed, but not in despair." In other words, we are at our wit's end and we don't know how to proceed. "Perplexed" is one of my favorite words in the New Testament. I could have it tattooed across my chest! I always seem to be in a state of perplexity, not understanding what God is doing in my life. It's OK to ask God, "What is going on?" Paul and his companions experienced that feeling many times—in Troas, Philippi, Athens, Corinth, and the prisons of Rome. But Paul did not live with a spirit of *despair*. He lived with the hope in this case that God would use his imprisonment to spread the good news of salvation. For example, God's calling was very clear to Paul. When you are called by God to minister in the major cities of the Roman Empire, however, it is very perplexing to end up in a Roman prison during the days of Nero, handcuffed to Roman guards for two years. And yet, it is because of that perplexing imprisonment that Paul wrote the four prison letters: Ephesians, Philippians, Colossians and Philemon. And it was because of that two-year prison term that he could write to the Christians in Philippi and inform them of the salvation of several servants within the palace.

"All the saints [in Rome] send you greetings, especially those who belong to Caesar's [Nero's] household."[21]

In his book *Knowing God*, J. I. Packer says that these perplexities are designed —

> to overwhelm us with a sense of our own inadequacy and to drive us to cling to him more closely....God fills our lives with troubles and perplexities...to ensure that we shall learn to hold him fast. The reason why the Bible spends so much of its time reiterating that God is a strong rock, a firm defense, a sure refuge and help for the weak is that God spends so much of his time bringing home to us that we are weak, both mentally and morally, and dare not trust ourselves to find or to follow the right road....God wants us to feel that our way through life is rough and perplexing, so that we may learn thankfully to lean on him. Therefore he takes steps to drive us out of self-confidence to trust in him, to wait upon the Lord.[22]

Paul continues, "[we are] persecuted, but not abandoned." He and his companions faced persecution many times for their commitment to Jesus. For example, on one occasion Paul was arrested for preaching the gospel in the temple area. He was brought before the high priest and the members of the Jewish supreme court and proclaimed, "I am on trial for the hope and resurrection of the dead!" The Pharisees and Sadducees got into such a heated argument over him that the Roman commander was afraid he would be torn to pieces and forced him out of the hands of the Jews. "The following night the Lord stood near Paul and said, 'Take courage! As you have testified about me in Jerusalem, so you must also testify in Rome.'"[23] Although Paul was falsely accused, beaten, and imprisoned for the sake of Christ, he never felt abandoned by his Lord.

Dietrich Bonhoeffer was a German pastor who was imprisoned by the Nazis for speaking out against Hitler's regime. Like Paul, he was eventually required to die for his faith in Jesus. He wrote in his *Letters and Papers from Prison*:

> I believe that God both can and will bring good out of evil. For that purpose he needs men who make the best use of everything. I believe God will give us all the power we need to resist in all times of distress. But he never gives it in advance, lest we should rely upon ourselves and not on him alone.[24]

A fellow prisoner described the last hours of Bonhoeffer's life in these words, demonstrating the wonderful truth as stated by Paul, "[we are] persecuted, but not abandoned."

> [On] Sunday 8th April, 1945, Pastor Bonhoeffer held a little service [for his fellow Christians].... He had hardly finished his last prayer when the door opened and two evil-looking men in civilian clothes came in and said: "Prisoner Bonhoeffer, get ready to come with us." Those words, "Come with us"—for all prisoners had come to mean one thing only—the scaffold.... We bade him good-bye—he drew me aside—"This is the end," he said. "For me the beginning of life." ...Next day, at Flossenbürg, he was hanged.[25]

Finally, Paul says, "[we are] struck down, but not destroyed." Many times Paul suffered the trauma of being suddenly smitten and cast down—rather like receiving an unexpected blow to the head. When he and his dear friend Barnabas were on their first missionary journey, they were having a successful ministry in the central Turkish towns of Lystra and Derbe. During this time, Paul healed a man who had been lame since birth. The people rejoiced and began to treat them like Greek gods. This immediately gave them an opportunity to preach the Good News that Jesus was the Messiah they had been looking for. In response, some of the Jews stoned Paul and left him for dead.[26] Paul probably remembered this sudden blow to the head as he was writing this letter to the Corinthians. He had been struck down by the enemies of Christ, but not destroyed.

At times the Lord allows deep blows to come into our lives in order to express his love and plan of redemption to those around us who need to hear of him and his love for them.[27] For example, in 1976 while Jack Crabtree was a pastor at Peninsula Bible Church, his two-year-old son, John David, swallowed an almond and choked to death. Jack and his wife Jody were emotionally struck down, but not destroyed, as Jack's words at the memorial service demonstrate.

> John David was more than a son, he was a miniature man who was our constant companion, a really, really good friend. We are going to miss him. But the incredible thing to both Jody and me, I think—I just stand first, unbelieving that it happened; I'm kind of numb and disbelieving—but the incredible thing is our whole reaction to this. There are times when we experience joy at what a magnificent, merciful, loving thing God has done. When I think about what a fat assignment my son got from the Lord, to come into the world and spend two years having nothing but utter joy...and then being taken home, I feel privileged to have had a son with that kind of an assignment. To be able to serve the Lord and go home to him as a full-grown and mature son now in his glory and to have missed a lot of the process that we have to go through—I'm privileged by that; what a merciful thing. Jody and I are both convinced that God has the right to take our son and that he has exercised that right; he has not done evil of John David, he has done good. But furthermore, he has not done evil of us, because John David is not our god, the Lord is our God. He is our life, he is the bread on which we feed, and he is the one on whom we are going to depend and find our fulfillment in the future.

All humanity is formed out of the dust. We are all "jars of clay," and as such we face afflictions, persecution and trauma—physically, emotionally and spiritually. When we become Christians, we are not suddenly lifted above the normal circumstances of life. We are the same clay jars, only now we contain the treasure of the life and power of the resurrected Christ within us. We have new strength to cope with the circumstances which God brings into our lives. We should no longer feel *crushed, despairing, abandoned* or *destroyed* when we choose to allow the Lord to live through us. We are enabled to see how God uses all these circumstances to his honor and glory, drawing us closer to him, teaching us to rely on him and bringing us into spiritual maturity.

The Goal of the Current Stress

Paul concludes this marvelous spiritual insight by showing the Corinthians that God is at work, calling a people for himself out of every nation. "We always carry around in our body the death of Jesus, so that the life of Jesus may also be revealed in our body." When the perfect Lamb of God died on the cross, all the sins of humanity were placed upon him—all the pride and self-reliance of man. The apostle explained this spiritual principle in his letter to the Christians in Rome. These men and women heard the Gospel and placed their faith in Jesus as the one who died in their place for their sins. They were saved from the wrath of God and the power of sin to rule their lives from that moment on.

The old life we had before we gave it to Christ with all its destructive habits, kept us enslaved to our own selfish desires and had great power and influence over us. But that power is broken once we invite the Son of God to become our Lord and Savior. He now lives within us and he has given us his Holy Spirit so that we can choose not to relapse into the habits of our old lifestyle. We now know that our new life in Jesus is no longer our own for we are now serving a new master.[28] As servants of Christ, we resist the desire to seek our rights and give in to our old feelings. Rather as servants of the new covenant, "jars of clay," we are to choose to allow the life of Jesus to be seen in our words and our actions, regardless of the outward circumstances. The result will be life out of death. People will see that we have weaknesses and problems just like they do. When they watch us living under the same stress they are under, however, they should see something different. We may physically look the same as we did before we gave our heart to Jesus, but our ability to handle life and our spiritual influence should be quite different.

Paul now shifts from situations in which Christians consciously choose to give up their rights, hopes and dreams so that Christ can live through them, to those in which he finds his life being used by God without his consent. "For we who are alive are always being given over to death for Jesus' sake, so that his life may be revealed in our mortal body." Notice the word *always*. This is a pattern for life. Near the end of this very letter Paul says,

> To keep me from becoming conceited...there was given me a thorn in my flesh, a messenger of Satan, to torment me. Three times I pleaded with the Lord to take it away from me. But he said to me, "My grace is sufficient for you, for my power is made perfect in weakness." Therefore I will boast all the more gladly about my weaknesses, so that Christ's power may rest on me. That is why, for Christ's sake, I delight in weaknesses, in insults, in hardships, in persecutions, in difficulties. For when I am weak, then I am strong.[29]

J. I. Packer summarized this principle as follows: "Through tribulations of pain and loss for Jesus' sake we enter into a thousand little deaths day by day, and through the ministry of the Spirit we rise out of those little deaths into constantly recurring experiences of risen life with Christ."[30]

When Paul says we are "given over to death," he is speaking of the death of our own hopes, dreams, and ambitions. Looking back over nearly four decades since that day in Jerusalem when I asked Jesus Christ to be my Lord, I am amazed at what has happened to the many personal ambitions I had before I came to know him. I had plans to be an artist, a radio disc jockey, a psychologist, a school teacher, or an actor. I had the super ego to believe that I could be anything I wanted to be if I worked hard—or all of the above if I worked even harder. But now some forty years later all those plans have been changed by my new master! What I really wanted was to be a *star* in my chosen field of endeavor, and he wanted me to be a servant for his sake. I can now say I take great joy in becoming a *servant* for Jesus' sake, but looking back, I can see I never would have *chosen* to become a servant.

"So then, death is at work in us, but life is at work in you." Because of the willingness of Paul and his disciples to die to the cry of the flesh and minister by the power of the Spirit in Corinth, many in that spiritually blind city came to know Jesus Christ as their Lord and Savior. Again, we need to come back to the basics: Jesus came to save sinners. He is calling out a people for his name's sake from every nation. He desires to use you and me, "jars of clay," as ministers of the new covenant, drawing on his life and power, dying to self—giving away our lives daily so that others can find new life in him.

Our Life is Not Our Own

We find freedom to cope when we realize that our very lives come from God and that he is the only one who can provide the strength we need in order to face the variety of situations placed before us in any given day.

> It is written: "I believed; therefore I have spoken." With that same spirit of faith we also believe and therefore speak, because we know that the one who raised the Lord Jesus from the dead will also raise us with Jesus and present us with you in his

presence. All this is for your benefit, so that the grace that is reaching more and more people may cause thanksgiving to overflow to the glory of God.[31]

Paul quotes Psalm 116: "I believed; therefore I have spoken." As the apostle experienced daily affliction, perplexity and persecution, he realized he was not the first believer to undergo stress. Here is how the psalmist described his experience:

> I love the Lord, for he heard my voice; he heard my cry for mercy. Because he turned his ear to me, I will call on him as long as I live. The cords of death entangled me, the anguish of the grave came upon me; I was overcome by trouble and sorrow. Then I called on the name of the Lord: "O Lord, save me!"[32]

The apostle remembers that the psalmist cried out to God in faith and asked God to save him. He believed that the invisible but ever-present Comforter and Deliverer would hear him in the midst of his present trial. By faith he spoke to God and waited. The psalmist continues:

> The Lord is gracious and righteous; our God is full of compassion. The Lord protects the simple hearted; when I was in great need, he saved me. Be at rest once more, O my soul, for the Lord has been good to you. For you, O Lord, have delivered my soul from death, my eyes from tears, my feet from stumbling, that I may walk before the Lord in the land of the living.[33]

Following his deliverance, the psalmist realized that sharing with the people of Jerusalem what had happened to him would greatly encourage them. Paul quotes from the psalm to encourage the Corinthians. "With that same spirit of faith," and in the same kind of pressure-cooker stress, "we also believe and therefore speak." He believed God could deliver him from all his enemies, both physical and spiritual, as well as afflictions, perplexities, persecutions and traumas, "because we know that the one who raised the Lord Jesus from the dead will also raise us with Jesus." That same God has the power to raise us out of our deadly situations.

This same God will also "present us with you in his presence." Here Paul steps back from the stress he is experiencing and looks ahead towards his and the Corinthians' spiritual perfection. All of their afflictions were worthwhile in light of the future when they would all meet together and be with Jesus forever. John the apostle encouraged the Christians at the end of the first century with these words: "Now the dwelling of God is with men, and he will live with them. They will be his people, and God himself will be with them and be their God. He will wipe every tear from their eyes. There will be no more death or mourning or crying or pain for the old order of things has passed away."[34]

"All this is for your benefit, so that the grace that is reaching more and more people may cause thanksgiving to overflow to the glory of God." God allowed stress to come into the Corinthians' lives so that his grace and love could be expressed through them toward a hopeless world. As they accepted Jesus into their lives, they found their hearts overflowing with thanksgiving to God for their new life. And the Corinthians' hearts were filled with joy as they finally realized what God was doing through their stressful experiences: saving their friends, neighbors and co-workers as they witnessed to them about Jesus.

This was not just a nice theory. Paul was speaking from experience, as the Corinthians well knew. I'm sure he had told them the story many times over the year-and-a-half he ministered with them. They probably thought back to his words when they became stressed and afraid of living as Christians in their corrupt community. The story: When Paul and his disciples came to Corinth for

the first time, they found an open door for the gospel, proclaiming to the Jewish community in the synagogue that Jesus was the
long-promised Messiah. In time, however, some of the religious
Jews became angry and opposed Paul. He finally left the synagogue and went, of all places, next-door to the home of Titius
Justus, a worshiper of God. Then the synagogue ruler, Crispus,
and his entire household believed in the Lord. Many of the
Corinthians who heard him also believed that Jesus was the
Christ and were baptized.

Now, you would think that this would have been a great time
to rejoice in the Lord—and perhaps some did. But something
else happened to Paul. For many good reasons, he became so
afraid of being physically harmed that he made plans to leave
town. The problem became so serious that Jesus made a visible
appearance to the apostle for the first time in twenty years. "One
night the Lord spoke to Paul in a vision: 'Do not be afraid, keep
on speaking, do not be silent. For I am with you and no one is
going to attack and harm you, because I have many people in this
city.' So Paul stayed for a year and a half teaching them the word
of God,"[35] before he moved on to Ephesus, Turkey.

As we look back on this passage, we can see that following in
the footsteps of Jesus is not always a smooth road. In fact, it is
usually a difficult, narrow road because we are called to speak
about him and his gospel of salvation and to be his servants for
the sake of hurting humanity. As we live our lives in these clay
jars, we come face to face with all kinds of pressures, perplexity,
and persecution. We give our lives away or God steps in to give
our lives away so that others may come to a vital relationship
with his Son. "So then, death is at work in us, but life is at work
in you." We are willing to give up our lives daily so that others
can experience the gift of eternal life. Where do we get the
strength to cope with all that pressure? It comes to each one of
us only when we realize that if our life comes from God, then
our strength must as well.

It is true that our new life from God sets us free at last to be like Jesus. At the same time, this new life can entail so many pressures that we are tempted to lose hope. Paul is about to share with us one of his greatest spiritual secrets that motivated him to remain faithful in the midst of incredible stress.

Chapter 7

Free at Last!
TO RESIST DISCOURAGEMENT

> **Now we see but a poor reflection as in a mirror; then we shall see face to face. Now I know in part; then I shall know fully, even as I am fully known.**
>
> **- Paul[1]**

Many times we find ourselves asking the eternal questions, such as: Where did I come from? Why am I here? And, do I really have to leave? Life is a mystery. It is a challenge to Christians and non-Christians alike. Our time on earth brings many seasons of joy and laughter. For most of us, life is a drive to fulfill personal hopes, dreams and ambitions. As Christians, we understand intellectually that our life is no longer our own.[2] At the same time, however, life is a process of learning how to let go of our own personal goals and line them up with the desires of our risen Lord Jesus.

Everyone experiences seasons of faded hopes, broken dreams and unfulfilled ambitions. Everyone has good days and bad days, sunny days and rainy days, times when we are up and times when we are down. It is the downers that we hate the most, the times when we find ourselves tempted to give in to discouragement. And yet discouragement destroys the freedom we have to live our lives and related to those around us as Jesus did on earth.

Discouragement immobilizes us. It robs us of our inner joy, peace, and sense of wholeness. It challenges the spiritual truth that we are free to be like our Lord. A leader of the human potential movement recently claimed to have developed a philosophy to avoid discouragement. He wrote, "I am bigger than anything that can happen to me. All these things—sorrow, misfortune, and suffering—are outside my door. I am in the house and I have the key." How I wish life were that simple! The folly of that kind of thinking leaves many adrift on a sea of uncertainty. The philosophy that says, "I am the captain of my fate," is unrealistic and absolutely untrue.

As followers of Jesus Christ, how can we resist the temptation to succumb when life as we understand it seems so discouraging? We are encouraged to turn to the word of God in order to see all of our present circumstances from a heavenly perspective. Jesus is the rock on which we take refuge when trying to avoid discouragement. In Paul's second letter to the Corinthians, we are discovering that the apostle has set forth many spiritual principles for living within this new freedom we have in Jesus Christ. As we have seen in this "thankful letter," Paul had very good reason to become discouraged: The false teachers were in Corinth attacking his name, ministry and authority as an apostle. He couldn't find Titus in Troas; he struggled with peace of mind, and journeyed on to Greece. He was tempted to become discouraged when he heard that the church elders in Corinth, his spiritual sons, were asking him to produce letters of recommendation before he could return for a visit. Then he remembered that his confidence to preach the gospel and live as a minister of the new covenant comes entirely from his risen Lord.

With this fresh perspective, Paul assures the Corinthians, "Therefore we do not lose heart."[3] Then he explains the focus they should have to avoid becoming discouraged while following Jesus on this earth. Paul encourages them to lift their eyes above the here and now and focus on the unseen, the eternal, and the priority of serving Jesus.

Fix Our Eyes on the Unseen

> Therefore we do not lose heart. Though outwardly
> we are wasting away, yet inwardly we are being
> renewed day by day. For our light and momentary
> troubles are achieving for us an eternal glory that
> far outweighs them all. So we fix our eyes not on
> what is seen, but on what is unseen. For what is
> seen is temporary, but what is unseen is eternal.[4]

Paul was a realist. When he wrote this letter, he was probably in his mid-fifties. His step was not as quick as in his youth; his eyesight was diminishing, and his once thick black hair was thinning and graying. As many of us do over time, he realized that we are but jars of clay, which God has designed to contain himself. We live on earth with the knowledge that these containers are crumbling away. But Paul says, "we do not lose heart"—we don't get discouraged—for he also knows that at the time of our physical death, God will give us a new eternal body. On the other hand, the person who has chosen to be "the captain of his fate" may in time realize that same truth of growing old and wasting away, but find himself facing an eternal loneliness as captain of his emptiness.

As we have seen, the joy of our new life begins the moment we place our faith in God's Son to forgive our sins. Our inner man becomes an eternal-life being that desires to serve God. And this new spiritual life does not waste away. On the contrary, we are being "renewed day by day"—not by activity, but by the presence of the Holy Spirit within, regardless of the condition of our temporary clay jar. In the words of Isaiah:

> Do you not know? Have you not heard? The
> Lord is the everlasting God, the Creator of the
> ends of the earth. He will not grow tired or
> weary, and his understanding no one can fathom.

He gives strength to the weary, and increases the power of the weak. Even youths grow tired and weary, and young men stumble and fall; but those who hope in the Lord will renew their strength. They will soar on wings like eagles; they will run and not grow weary, they will walk and not be faint.[5]

When I was a college student in Pennsylvania, I went on a church weekend retreat to Ocean City, New Jersey. On Saturday afternoon we put together a softball game on the warm sand by the water. Our "field" was just in front of a stately old beach hotel with a long open porch. An 80-year-old friend, whom we affectionately called "Nana," came out and sat in one of the rocking chairs on the porch to watch us play. While waiting for our turn at bat, several of us sat on the steps and talked with her. At the seventh inning stretch I asked how she liked the game. "I love it," she said. "In fact, I was thinking, if it weren't for this body, I'd be playing second base!" She was keenly aware that her physical body was aging, but her spirit was as youthful as ever.

The factor that kept Paul from becoming discouraged was the knowledge that "our light and momentary troubles are achieving for us an eternal glory that far outweighs them all." The apostle weighs his afflictions on one side of an imaginary set of scales, and the glory to come on the other. He seeks to understand life from God's point of view; to look over God's shoulder, as it were, and see the spiritual realities behind his present circumstances. As we have seen, the apostle and his companions had experienced beatings, imprisonment and shipwrecks—but all of these were achieving an eternal glory that would far outweigh them all. Though it is somewhat of a mystery to us, these hardships in our lives are part of God's plan for our maturing process.

Paul contrasts the terms *momentary* and *eternal, light* and *weight, troubles* and *glory*. In the Greek language in which Paul wrote, the word weight carried the idea of authority, influence, and responsibility. He understands that these afflictions were designed by God to prepare us for responsibility in eternity. Be encouraged: God is at work in these jars of clay. We are not just getting old. The *Jerusalem Bible* translates this verse: "Yes, the troubles which are soon over, though they weigh little, train us for the carrying of a weight of eternal glory which is out of all proportion to them." God is using all the stresses, the pain, the aging, the momentary troubles to train us for something better. This view stands in sharp contrast to the modern view of secularism which teaches people to live only for the present because there is no other life. As Christians, however, our character and actions on earth have eternal consequences.

This idea goes hand-in-hand with some of the promises Jesus made to his disciples about a future reward. Speaking of his coming kingdom, he said to the Twelve, "You are those who have stood by me in my trials. And I confer on you a kingdom, just as my Father conferred one on me, so that you may eat and drink at my table in my kingdom and sit on thrones, judging the twelve tribes of Israel."[6] He told his disciples on the Mount of Olives how he would deal with his disciples when he comes again: "Who then is the faithful and wise servant, whom the master has put in charge of the servants in his household to give them their food at the proper time? It will be good for that servant whose master finds him doing so when he returns. I tell you the truth, he will put him in charge of all his possessions."[7] This same principle can be seen in the parable of the faithful servants who used their talents and invested them wisely for the master when he was away. When he returned, the master said to them: "Well done, good and faithful servant! You have been faithful with a few things; I will put you in charge of many things. Come and share your master's happiness!"[8]

On the night that he was betrayed, the Lord Jesus gave his disciples a command "to go and bear fruit."[9] Paul picks up on the spiritual principle that how we live here on earth affects how and in what position of responsibility we shall live in eternity.

He tells the Corinthians that they need to be very aware that the way they handle lawsuits against each other cannot be based on the principles of this world. Instead, their actions should be based on the spiritual principles of the world to come because they will be placed in positions of authority when they come back with Jesus to judge the world as well as angels.[10]

It should be a great comfort to us to know that God is getting us ready to serve with him in eternity and that he is using the trials and stresses of this life to bring us to spiritual maturity. The fact that who I am and what I do affect my eternal weight of glory, should encourage my heart that this life isn't "all there is." Our Lord understood that spiritual principle in his life and then his death: first the cross, then the crown. The writer to the Hebrews wrote in this same theme: "Let us fix our eyes on Jesus, the author and perfecter of our faith, who for the joy set before him endured the cross, scorning its shame, and sat down at the right hand of the throne of God. Consider him who endured such opposition from sinful men, so that you will not grow weary and lose heart."[11]

In his book *The Eternal Weight of Glory*, C. S. Lewis built on this idea that we will be given responsibilities to serve with Jesus in heaven. He wrote that the Scriptures promise us:

> firstly, that we shall be with Christ; secondly, that we shall be like Him; thirdly, with an enormous wealth of imagery, that we shall have "glory"; fourthly, that we shall, in some sense, be fed or feasted or entertained; and, finally, that we shall have some sort of official position in the universe—ruling cities, judging angels, being pillars of God's temple.[12]

Paul is reminding his readers that our life and our good works done in the power of the Holy Spirit and to the glory of God are important in the life to come. Everything that happens to the Christian in this life is adding up. First the suffering, then the glory. When we have that perspective, how can we be discouraged, disheartened and complaining? Everything is on schedule—God's schedule.

Paul concludes, "We fix our eyes not on what is seen, but on what is unseen. For what is seen is temporary, but what is unseen is eternal." The key to understanding life is to live by faith in Christ, for faith is trusting in unseen realities.

Eugene H. Peterson again provides helpful insight into this spiritual principle in *The Message*, his modern paraphrase of the New Testament:

> So we're not giving up. How could we! Even though on the outside it often looks like things are falling apart on us, on the inside, where God is making new life, not a day goes by without his unfolding grace. These hard times are small potatoes compared to the coming good times, the lavish celebration prepared for us. There's far more here than meets the eye. The things we see now are here today, gone tomorrow. But the things we can't see now will last forever.[13]

Fix Our Minds on Our Eternal Home

In addition to looking at the unseen realities of life, Paul wants his readers to have an eternal perspective.

> Now we know that if the earthly tent we live in is destroyed, we have a building from God, an eternal house in heaven, not built by human hands. Meanwhile we groan, longing to be clothed with our heavenly dwelling, because when we are clothed, we will not be found naked. For while we are in this tent, we groan and are burdened, because we do not wish to be unclothed but to be clothed with our heavenly dwelling, so that what

is mortal may be swallowed up by life. Now it is
God who has made us for this very purpose and
has given us the Spirit as a deposit, guaranteeing
what is to come.[14]

The apostle reminds the Corinthians that they are aliens on
this earth following in the footsteps of Abraham, Moses, and
Jesus. He has just talked about how we are eternal beings living
on this earth as "clay pots" to contain the life of Christ. Now as
a tentmaker himself, he wants the Corinthians to see that in
light of eternity, our bodies can also be compared to tents in
which we "camp out" until we are called home to be with our
Lord.

First-century Greek and Roman philosophers regarded their
bodies in a much different light. Epictetus, the Greek Stoic
philosopher, said of himself, "Thou art a poor soul, burdened
with a corpse." Seneca, a Roman philosopher and author of
tragedies, wrote, "I am a higher being and born for higher
things than to be the slave of my body which I look upon as only
a shackle put upon my freedom.... In so detestable a habitation
dwells the free soul."[15]

In contrast to the thinking of his contemporaries, Paul's
understanding here is that once God calls believers to join him
in eternity, he simply "breaks camp" and folds up our earthly
tent. When our tent is folded up in physical death, our inner
man will receive a permanent eternal home formed by the hand
of God, a house designed to hold our eternal soul and spirit. A
body of some kind is essential to our personality.[16] Peter, James
and John saw Moses and Elijah wearing their eternal bodies on
the Mount of Transfiguration. These three disciples watched as
Jesus took off his "tent," which he had been wearing since his
conception, put on his spiritual body, and joined the prophets of
old in eternity. Then he stepped back into time and put his
earthly "tent" back on until his physical death on the cross.[17] At
his resurrection he again put on his eternal body forever and

promised all who believe in him as Son of the living God that they too would receive a new body.

Paul goes on to discuss our natural desire to have our perfect resurrection bodies now. "We groan, longing to be clothed with our heavenly dwelling, because when we are clothed, we will not be found naked. For while we are in this tent, we groan...." During the Depression my family had to leave our home and move onto a friend's farm. All he could provide for our family of four was a tent pitched in a grove of trees. This was no camping trip. The tent was our only home until a tree fell on it during a storm. I remember my mother sitting on a soaked cot with the tent ripped to pieces at her feet in the mud and rain. She wept for her home, which we had lost because we could not pay the mortgage. In this way we groan for our eternal houses. We do not want to be found naked; that is, to be disembodied spirits. We long for our covering—to be clothed with a resurrection body. We long to be like Jesus is now.

What really happens when a believer dies physically? One popular idea is called *soul sleep*: When you die you fall into a deep sleep and are unaware of time until the Lord returns. Then you are awakened and given your new resurrection body. However, when the thief dying on the cross asked Jesus, "Remember me when you come in your kingdom"—acknowledging him as Messiah—Jesus replied, "*Today* you will be with me in paradise."[18]

I call another idea the "rent-a-suit" theory. Some think that our tent is placed in the ground and our eternal spirit is given a rent-a-suit to wear in heaven. When the Lord returns to earth, he will collect all the rent-a-suits from believers who have physically died. Then he will give eternal houses to them as well as to the believers who are still alive on earth.[19] This comes easily to us because we are caught in time and space, and all of our thinking is locked into a sequence with a beginning, middle, and end. But from God's eternal perspective, everything happens all at once. We can't bring time into eternity.

A third idea I would term *instant* resurrection bodies. Jesus' resurrection body is our best example that from God's point of view, believers immediately receive their eternal house as soon as they fold their tent on earth. Moses and Elijah were wearing their eternal houses when they met Jesus at the Transfiguration. It appears, further, from many other Scriptures that from God's perspective, which is not bound by time, we will all arrive in eternity at the same time—Adam, Moses, Elijah, Paul, Peter, Augustine, Luther, Calvin, you, and I. The writer of Hebrews lists the saints placed by God in the Hall of Faith, and then adds, "These were all commended for their faith, yet none of them received what had been promised. God had planned something better for us so that only together with us would they be made perfect."[20]

"Now he who prepared us for this very purpose is God, who gave to us the Spirit as a pledge," Paul continues. We owe our existence to God, who gives us our resurrection body so that we may reign with Christ forever. And God in Christ has given his church, his bride, an engagement ring—the presence and witness of his Holy Spirit. As Paul wrote to the Ephesians, when we believed, we were "marked in him with a seal, the promised Holy Spirit, who is a deposit guaranteeing our inheritance until the redemption of those who are God's possession—to the praise of his glory."[21] Every time we become aware of the Holy Spirit's activity we should take heart, because it is a reminder of God's promise of an eternal home.

Fix Our Hearts on Pleasing Christ

Another key to remaining encouraged even in the difficulties of life is to keep our focus on obeying God and pleasing him.

Therefore we are always confident and know that as long as we are at home in the body we are away from the Lord. We live by faith, not by sight. We

are confident, I say, and would prefer to be away
from the body and at home with the Lord. So we
make it our goal to please him, whether we are at
home in the body or away from it. For we must
all appear before the judgment seat of Christ,
that each one may receive what is due him for the
things done while in the body, whether good
or bad.[22]

The resurrected Christ is now present and reigning in our
hearts. The Holy Spirit lives within us, and though we sense
that our body is wasting away, in this time of "tenting" we live
by faith, not by sight. Faith is the key to living out our new life
with Jesus. He promised his disciples, and us as well, that
although we have to "tent" on earth for a season, and thus be
away from his visible presence, we will one day see him face to
face. That is why he told his disciples in the Upper Room, "Do
not let your hearts be troubled. Trust in God; trust also in me.
In my Father's house there are many rooms; if it were not so,
I would have told you. I am going there to prepare a place for
you.... I will come back and take you to be with me that you also
may be where I am."[23]

"Therefore we are always confident ... and would prefer to be
away from the body and at home with the Lord." Paul is saying,
"You know, I would love to leave the trauma of this fallen and
evil world, with all its sorrow, grief, pain and disappointments,
but I'm not in control of my life or the time of my 'tenting.'"
Moses wrote, "The length of our days is seventy years—or
eighty, if we have the strength.... Teach us to number our days
aright, that we may gain a heart of wisdom."[24] In other words,
buy up the time because this life is not all there is. Use God's
wisdom, love and knowledge. Don't waste your life on things
that are passing away.

The apostle continues, "We make it our goal to please him,
whether we are at home in the body or away from it." Jesus

taught this principle to his disciples over and over as he sought to obey his Father. "I tell you the truth, the Son can do nothing by himself; he can do only what he sees his Father doing, because whatever the Father does the Son also does. For the Father loves the Son and shows him all he does."[25] Jesus told them that he did nothing on his own initiative, but always sought his Father's will.[26] He assured them that even the things he said came straight from his Father.[27]

Pleasing God, then, depends on our relationship to his Son, Jesus. As Augustine said, "Love God and do what you please." If you love God you'll want to do exactly what he desires.

Paul was also delighted to make it his goal to please the Lord Jesus, whether in the physical body he had on earth or his resurrection body he would be given in heaven. This was possible because his new life in Christ had already begun at the time of his salvation on the Damascus road and it would continue on into eternity. As a new creature in Christ, the apostle knew while on earth that he had been given the power of the Holy Spirit to choose between pleasing himself or Jesus. So Paul said that he made it his ambition to please the Lord. That means as Jesus depended on his Father's resources while on earth, we too should draw on his power moment by moment to accomplish his will.

The Judgment Seat

Now we come to the motivating factor behind Paul's ambition to please the Lord with his life and his time: "For we must all appear before the judgment seat of Christ, that each one may receive what is due him for the things done while in the body, whether good or bad." In Corinth there was a place called the *bema* or judgment seat, where official business was conducted and justice was dispensed. You can still see the remains of the *bema* in the old city of Corinth. Paul had very vivid memories of it as he was once dragged before this judgment seat on false charges.[28]

The Christian community is confused about God's judgments. There is the *judgment of our sins on the cross*. Jesus was willing to go to the cross and take on himself the full wrath of God against our sin. He died in our place. If we place our faith in him as our substitute, our sins are not only forgiven, but never remembered again, a truth which God promised all believers in the new covenant.

There is the *judgment of the nations*.[29] The nations will one day appear before Christ and be evaluated according to how they have treated Israel during the great tribulation period. There is the *great white throne judgment*,[30] in which all who are not found in "the book of life" are cast into the lake of fire. This is called the second death. Then, finally, there is the *judgment seat of Christ*, designed for Christians. Paul had explained this to the Corinthians earlier:

> By the grace God has given me, I laid a founda-
> tion as an expert builder, and someone else is
> building on it. But each one should be careful
> how he builds. For no one can lay any foundation
> other than the one already laid, which is Jesus
> Christ. If any man builds on this foundation
> using gold, silver, costly stones, wood hay, straw,
> his work will be shown for what it is, because the
> Day will bring it to light. It will be revealed with
> fire, and the fire will test the quality of each man's
> work."[31]

It is this present and future judgment that motivates Paul. This is not the judgment of a person's sins, for they have been dealt with. Nevertheless, sin does have an effect on our service. Our present sin takes time and energy away from serving the Lord. We can be open to having the Holy Spirit convict us now of wrong motives and then we will not have to deal with them in eternity. But keep in mind that the judgment seat of Jesus Christ is open 24 hours a day, each day of our life on earth.

This evaluation has to do with the motives behind our good works: Did we choose to do them in our own strength, or in the power of the Holy Spirit?

If our good works are done in our own strength, with selfish motives, they are seen by God as wood, hay and straw and will be burned up. If they are done in the power of the Spirit and to the glory of the Lord, he views them as gold, silver, and precious stones. As Paul further explains to the Corinthians: "If what he [the Christian] builds survives, he will receive his reward. If it is burned up, he will suffer loss; he himself will be saved, but only as one escaping through the flames."[32]

A wonderful example of living and serving God in the Spirit can be seen when Jesus was sitting with his disciples in the Temple area.

> As he looked up, Jesus saw the rich putting their gifts into the temple treasury. He also saw a poor widow put in two very small copper coins. "I tell you the truth," he said, "this poor widow has put in more than all the others. All these people gave their gifts out of their wealth; but she out of her poverty put in all she had to live on."[33]

Paul has already asserted that we should walk by faith, drawing on Christ's power for everything we do. As he went through life, he discovered that there were times when he slipped back into his old habit of relying on his own strength. When he became aware of these motives by the convicting work of the Holy Spirit, he would evaluate them and confess them. He would then go on depending on the Lord for godly motives in his words and actions in the future. Later Paul would write to the Corinthians to let them know that at times he is not always sure of his motives. In the immediate context, he was dealing with people who thought he may not have been faithful in sharing the secret things of God. "I do not even judge myself. My conscience is clear, but that does not make me innocent. It is the Lord who judges me. Therefore judge nothing before the appointed time; wait till the Lord comes. He will bring to light what is hidden in darkness and will expose the motives of men's hearts. At that time each will receive his praise from God."[34] In a real sense Paul knew that the judgment seat of Christ was always in session.

As it was with Paul, so it is with us, "for we must all appear before the judgment seat of Christ." At that time, the issue will not be salvation, but reward and loss. It will be a time not only of judgment but also of encouragement. And it will be a time of official business, for the judgment is necessary for the appointment of places of rulership and authority with Christ, the King of Kings and Lord of Lords.

How can we remain encouraged so we can be free to be like Jesus in the midst of a very discouraging society? Paul revealed the spiritual secret of his consistent spirit of encouragement. We need to fix our eyes on the unseen. Physically we are decaying, but our inner person is being renewed day by day. The trials and struggles of this life are producing for us an eternal weight of glory, and it is becoming clearer every new day as God gives us the spiritual eyes to see that this world is growing strangely dim in the light of the glory of our Lord Jesus. We also need to fix our minds on our eternal home. As we live our lives by faith and not by sight, we realize now that life is not just camping out in a tent on this earth. We are looking forward to our new eternal house. Finally, we need to fix our hearts on pleasing Christ, whether here on earth or later in heaven. We are all presently standing before the judgment seat of Christ. The motives behind our good works will be judged, determining our eternal place of responsibility with Christ Jesus.

Was Paul discouraged at the end of his tenting season? Not at all, according to his words to Timothy, written just before his death in Rome. He was still free from disappointment, and within a few weeks he would become free at last to enter into the visible presence of the Lord Jesus, whom he loved and served faithfully.

> I am already being poured out like a drink offering, and the time has come for my departure. I have fought the good fight, I have finished the race, I have kept the faith. Now there is in store for me the crown of righteousness, which the Lord, the righteous Judge, will award to me on that day—and not only to me, but also to all who have longed for his appearing."[35]

Chapter 8

Free-at Last!
TO LIVE FOR JESUS

You are not your own; you were bought at a price.
- Paul[1]

At a dinner party in Southern California several years ago, I met a man in whom I immediately sensed a kindred spirit. After an evening of delightful conversation, my new friend invited my wife and me to his home, which he had been working on for several years. We gladly agreed to make a quick visit the following morning before our flight home.

As we drove up to his house, we immediately noticed that it was really an unfinished mansion. We parked in front of the large, hand-carved Spanish gates. An incomplete ten-foot-high concrete wall surrounded the entire property. Our new friend met us at the gates: "Welcome to my Waterloo, my field of absolute defeat. Welcome to my failure." As we toured the house, he told us the history behind his words. Thirteen years earlier, he had dedicated himself to building a mansion for his wife. He had visited Europe to research plans, brought in craftsmen from Mexico, and even built a custom tool-shop. He pointed out that the ceiling beams and the gates were hand-carved. In the midst of what he called this "obsession," his wife finally said, "You are a bore." Then she walked out on him, taking with her one of his contractors and leaving him with his "Waterloo."

We felt immense compassion for him. He had lost his way. He didn't understand life. Since we had to leave to catch our plane, I told him I would write him a letter explaining how Jesus Christ could change him and give him new life, life as it was intended to be lived by Christ's resurrection power. I did write that letter, and shortly afterwards I received word that he had been rushed to surgery for a bypass operation. I called him in the hospital and asked if he had read my letter. He said he was too weak to open it. A few weeks later, the friends who had introduced us phoned with the sad news that our mutual friend had committed suicide. As far as we know, this man went into eternity without any living hope.

Unfortunately, many people go through life with no real hope. It's amazing to me how many people think that just because they are breathing, they are living. From God's perspective, however, they don't have a clue as to what life is all about. In this second letter to the young Christian church at Corinth, the apostle Paul sought to answer for his spiritual children the same type of question that so many men and women around us are asking today: What is my purpose for living? Paul lets us in on the secrets of his life and ministry.

Paul reminded the Corinthians that his main purpose in life was to please his Lord and to take every opportunity to share his message of salvation with anyone willing to listen.

> Since, then, we know what it is to fear the Lord,
> we try to persuade men. What we are is plain
> to God, and I hope it is also plain to your con-
> science. We are not trying to commend ourselves
> to you again, but are giving you an opportunity to
> take pride in us, so that you can answer those who
> take pride in what is seen rather than in what is in
> the heart. If we are out of our mind, it is for the
> sake of God; if we are in our right mind, it is for
> you.[2]

After sharing with his Corinthian friends that his ambition is to please the Lord, Paul reveals the motivating factors that kept him on target. We have already discussed the motivation of the judgment seat of Christ. Now we see that Paul is also motivated by the fear of the Lord.

Motivated by the Fear of the Lord

Paul wants the Corinthians to know that his heart is filled with the "the fear of the Lord." Paul has been acquainted with this truth since his childhood from hearing the rabbis recite over and over: "And now, O Israel, what does the Lord your God ask of you, but to fear the Lord your God, to walk in all his ways, to love him, to serve the Lord your God with all your heart and with all your soul?"[3] It is one thing to hear this great truth and keep it in your mind, but once Paul came face to face with the risen Messiah on the road to Damascus, that truth moved from his mind to his heart. He was filled with awe not only for God, but also for what he was willing to do on behalf of a dying world.

This respect gave Paul a strong desire to persuade men and women in Corinth to come to know his Lord. This fear of God kept him ministering by the power of the Holy Spirit in sincerity, with his motives open before God and the Corinthians. Paul says he is seeking to live an honest life in the sight of God and men. He is not trying to hide his true message as the false teachers had been doing since he left town. He and his team were seeking to live with spiritual integrity so that God could produce eternal results through them.

Paul's spiritual zeal for the Lord caused the false teachers and the nominal Christians to think that he was insane or looking for a way to get invited back to Corinth. But Paul responds, "If we are beside ourselves, it is for God; if we are of sound mind, it is for you." In other words, he says, "Our motive is to honor God even if it makes us look crazy. But if you realize that we are indeed sane, then please understand that our goal is to serve you." He resolved to live transparently before God and man and allow the accusations to fall where they may. He would not be distracted from his goal.

Motivated by the Love of Christ

The other motivating factor behind Paul's ambition was Jesus' love.

> For Christ's love compels us, because we are con-
> vinced that one died for all, and therefore all
> died. And he died for all, that those who live
> should no longer live for themselves but for him
> who died for them and was raised again.[4]

The love of Jesus guarded him, controlled him and sent him out. He was overwhelmed by the self-sacrificial love of the Messiah for his people Israel, the Gentiles, and the foremost of all sinners, himself.[5]

Paul defines the depth of God's love: "…we are convinced that one died for all." He expounded on this concept in his letter to the Roman believers: "Therefore, just as sin entered the world through one man [Adam], and death through sin, and in this way death came to all men, because all sinned…."[6] Here lies the root problem of all humanity, though few people will acknowledge it. From God's viewpoint, we are all dead and alienated from him.[7]

Paul also wrote to the Romans: "But God demonstrates his own love for us in this: While we were still sinners, Christ died for us."[8] It was because of that love that the alienation between God and man could be healed. Left to his own devices, man cannot save himself or restore fellowship with God. Jesus' death on the cross covers all the sinners in every generation, for "he died for all." Everyone who hears that good news and is willing to place his faith in Jesus as his sin-bearer and mediator between God and himself discovers that the best news is yet to come:

"...that those who live should no longer live for themselves but for him who died for them and was raised again." Because Jesus was raised from the dead by his Father, all who place their faith in him are also raised to a new life filled with joy, peace and wholeness. Now in the midst of the struggle in which our former lifestyle and worldly habits still influence our memories, we can choose to allow him to enable us to resist the many temptations that once arose from our selfish hopes and desires. In our new resurrected life, we can choose to live to please our new Lord instead of ourselves.

On a recent men's retreat, I roomed with an old friend. We had served the Lord together on many different projects and shared many dinners together with our wives. On the last night of our retreat, the speaker addressed our need to be like Jesus and to pray about everything before we do anything, say anything or go anywhere. This message convicted my friend deeply, and he told me that over his years as a Christian he had not developed that kind of a lifestyle. The reason he neglected to pray was because he felt talented and capable in so many areas that it rarely occurred to him that he should pray about them. That evening, however, he told me that he was going to pray that the Lord would change his heart. He wanted the Lord to teach him to pray about what he was going to say and do and where he was going to go. Today my friend is a man who has been set free to continue to grow spiritually and think and live like our risen Lord.

Free to Live as a New Creation

Why am I here on this earth and what is my purpose for living? Paul tells the Corinthians—and us—to remember that we are no longer to live for ourselves, but instead to live as a new creation.

So from now on we regard no one from a worldly point of view. Though we once regarded Christ

in this way, we do so no longer. Therefore, if anyone is in Christ, he is a new creation; the old has
gone, the new has come![9]

Having been set free from our old nature because of our new
relationship with Jesus, we become new creatures with a new
heart and new eyes to see people as Jesus sees them. He sets us
free from prejudice, bigotry, and self-righteousness: Jews,
Gentiles, masters, slaves, men, women and little children have
unique value in the sight of God because all are created in his
image. Jesus frees us from judging others by their outward
appearance—money, status, speech—from placing people in
boxes and then stamping them as approved or rejected. He sets
us free to see that they are valuable and worthy to hear the good
news.

In a store recently, I noticed a giant of a man with long hair
and a ragged beard. He was wearing a tank top and I could see
that his upper body was covered with tattoos. I thought to
myself, "What a mess! This guy doesn't know what life is all
about." I wanted to walk away from him because he didn't look
like me or act like me. Actually, he was a threat to me, and I don't
like to be around people who threaten me. I want to feel safe. But
Paul would say that as Christians with new eyes, we should look
at this man as one whom God loves and one who may have need
of a savior. And as people with new hearts we should have a great
compassion for him and if possible, seek an opportunity to tell
him the good news of Jesus's love. On the other hand, he may be
a Christian and his outward appearance may simply be a style he
has chosen, for all the right reasons.

Paul seems to indicate that before he became a Christian, he
himself saw Jesus. He may have stood amidst the crowd on Palm
Sunday when Jesus rode into Jerusalem on a colt as the long-
awaited Messiah and Prince of Peace. Paul may have seen the
people laying down palm leaves before him while they sang:
"Hosanna to the Son of David; Blessed is he who comes in the

name of the Lord; Hosanna in the highest!"[10] Or he may have been among the chief priests and scribes in the temple area when they watched Jesus chase out the moneychangers and then heal the blind and lame as the children cried out, "Hosanna to the Son of David," causing the priests and scribes to become indignant. At that time he may have seen Jesus as a blasphemer and political rebel. This may have been the seed of hatred that caused Paul (then Saul) to persecute the new body of Jewish believers even as far away as the city of Damascus. But he came face-to-face with the resurrected Jesus on the Damascus road (some twenty years before he wrote this letter) and finally saw him for the first time as his long-awaited Messiah. Ever since that day, his spiritual eyes had been opened to see all men and women as created in the image of God and greatly loved by him.

Paul concludes, "Therefore if anyone is in Christ, he is a new creation; the old has gone, the new has come!" The word "new" here is the same word used in the phrase "new covenant," which we saw earlier. It means new in form or quality of life. This *new creation* can occur only when a person places their faith in Jesus as Lord and Savior. Only God can take a person dead in his sins and make him alive in Christ.[11] In explaining the idea to Nicodemus, Jesus told him he must be "born again." When Paul wrote his first letter to the Corinthians, he remembered that when he first came to their city, he found them enslaved to sexual immorality, idolatry, greed, stealing, drunkenness, slandering and swindling each other.

The fruit of this new creation is that "the old has gone." In the immediate context, Paul was thinking about his fleshly view of Jesus in his humanity, but in the fuller context he was thinking of how he had previously judged all men and women. He had related to them based on their position, power, wealth, gender, race or religion, because that is the way he had regarded himself, as we saw in his list of credentials in his letter to the Philippians. When he became a new creation by the hand of God, he began his spiritual transformation in which "new things have come."[12]

The apostle Peter contrasted the old life before Christ and the new life with Christ when he wrote to the second generation of Christians in Asia around 62 AD. He told them that Jesus lived his whole life for the will of God. Then he challenged them: "For you have spent enough time in the past doing what pagans choose to do—living in debauchery, lust, drunkenness, orgies, carousing and detestable idolatry. They think it strange that you do not plunge with them into the same flood of dissipation, and they heap abuse on you. But they will have to give account to him who is ready to judge the living and the dead." Then he went on to encourage the new Christians to live in the truth that "the new has come," by praying for, loving and being hospitable to each other and finding their spiritual gifts and using them to the glory of God.[13]

Everyone is in different stages of this growth process. Let us not judge others, because God is at work. We are filled with hope because we know that he will finish the work which he began in us. We are sometimes in a hurry with each other, aren't we? We love to see people come to know Jesus, but at the same time we want him to mature them quickly so that we can get along with them better. Each individual is on a different time schedule, according to God's design. We need to be very patient with each other as God is patient with us.

Free to Share the Message of Reconciliation

With our new life comes new responsibility, Paul continues. We can now share the good news that God is not mad at us, but that he loves us so much that he was willing to provide a way for us to be reconciled to him.

> All this is from God, who reconciled us to himself through Christ and gave us the ministry of recon-ciliation: that God was reconciling the world to himself in Christ, not counting men's sins against them. And he has committed to us the message of reconciliation.[14]

While the sins of all of humanity have been dealt with on the cross by the death of Jesus, we are told elsewhere in Scripture that the Holy Spirit has come to convict the world of sin, which is, according to the words of Jesus, that "they do not believe in Me."[15] Many people believe that they will not get into heaven because of all their sins, but Paul tells us they have been forgiven. The only issue between man and God is, "What is your relationship with my Son Jesus? Did you place your faith in him, the only one who can deal with your sins against Me and the only one who can open the door back into fellowship with me? I desire reconciliation with you. Do you desire reconciliation with me?"

Paul re-emphasizes this thought: "And he has committed to us the message of reconciliation." What an incredible God we have! What a fabulous ministry and message! As God's children, we have a responsibility by his power to spread the good news. He calls us to take this wonderful message of salvation to a world filled with hopeless, dying people, living in a spiritual famine, alienated from God. As new creatures in Christ and ministers of reconciliation, we can tell our friends, our family as well as strangers that if they place their faith in Jesus, they will be reconciled to the Father and become children of God. The Father's righteous and holy demands have been satisfied in the death of his Son for the sins of mankind. The door between us and God is open again. We can go home! We are restored to daily fellowship with our creator and savior. That is great news! This is a great message of love!

How are we called to share the word of reconciliation? Francis of Assisi wrote some eight hundred years ago: "Preach the gospel all the time; if necessary use words."[16]

Free to be Ambassadors for Christ

Since God has given us the ministry and message of reconciliation, Paul calls us to be ambassadors for Christ.

> We are therefore Christ's ambassadors, as though
> God were making his appeal through us. We
> implore you on Christ's behalf: Be reconciled to
> God. God made him who had no sin to be sin for
> us, so that in him we might become the righteous-
> ness of God. As God's fellow workers we urge you
> not to receive God's grace in vain. For he says, "In
> the time of my favor I heard you, and in the day of
> salvation I helped you." I tell you, now is the time
> of God's favor, now is the day of salvation.[17]

An ambassador is a diplomatic official of the highest rank, accredited as a representative of his country in a foreign nation. He is appointed to reflect the character and policies of his leaders and people. In the same way, God has appointed us to represent his kingdom and communicate his message of good news in a foreign environment. An ambassador represents one who is not personally present. We are (present tense) ambassadors for Christ, representing One who is present but invisible. Our task is to deliver the good news that God wants to reconcile the world to himself, and not count people's sins against them. Once they accept that truth, they become, in Christ, all that God requires a person to be, all they could never be in themselves.

A number of years ago, I had a powerful experience which illus-trates this spiritual principle. On a prison ministry trip through Colombia, I was part of a team that visited the Acacias Prison, south of Bogota. When our small bus reached the prison grounds, we unloaded our musical equipment and boxes of literature. As the guards instructed, we carried our supplies across a rickety swinging bridge over a fast-moving river, and then struggled uphill for about a mile. Once inside, we had the privilege of sharing the good news of Jesus Christ through singing and teach-ing from the Bible. Most of the men in the audience looked on with lifeless, hopeless eyes. After the meeting, we toured the prison, a hellhole of cells surrounding a courtyard. As we were preparing to leave, the guards ordered some prisoners to help us carry our equipment back down the hill and across that perilous swinging bridge.

At the bus, one of the prisoners approached me. Surrounded by heavily armed guards, this handsome young man humbly asked through our interpreter, "Sir, would you redeem me?" I turned to the guard and asked, "What is he talking about?" The guard explained that prisoners who have served their sentence can't be released from prison until they or someone else can pay a ransom price to *redeem* them. (This money is supposed to go to the crime victim.) I asked the guard how much money it would take to redeem this man. "One thousand pesos," he replied.

I had about 200 pesos in my pocket and easily rounded up 800 more from the other members of our team. I then asked how much this represented in American currency. Eight dollars, someone answered. "Eight dollars! How much would it take to redeem all the prisoners here?" I inquired. This man was the only prisoner eligible to be redeemed at that time, so I handed the guard the 1000 pesos. The former prisoner boarded our bus and we drove him to freedom. Once outside the main gate, the ex-prisoner humbly walked to the back of the bus and said, "*Muchas gracias, señor, por mi redención*." ("Thank you, sir, for my redemption.")

I had a brief opportunity to share with this man some words that Peter wrote to a suffering community of Christians. He was not writing about a physical redemption from prison, but about the need for all men and women to experience spiritual redemption from sin. "For you know that it was not with perishable things such as silver or gold [or pesos] that you were redeemed from the empty way of life..., but with the precious blood of Christ, a lamb without blemish or defect."[18]

That Colombian prisoner approached me by faith, with the hope that I would have 1000 pesos to redeem him. I was delighted to serve as an ambassador for Christ in that way. God is still asking all of us to approach his Son Jesus with the same humble faith of that prisoner, for he has already willingly and lovingly paid our redemption price with his blood. Because of his resurrection from the dead, Jesus is now willing and able to deliver us not only from our sin, but also from the rule of Satan and the evil and destructive forces of this world.

The Ultimate Challenge

Finally, Paul addresses his spiritual children like a father who wants them to understand the fullness of their salvation and the joy they can experience if they choose to trust God for every moment of every day. "We urge you not to receive God's grace in vain." Paul appeals to his readers to get in step with his plan of redemption. As you have received the gift of salvation, share that truth with all those who have never heard about it.

Like the Corinthian Christians, all followers of Jesus have received the grace of God. Our salvation is wholly undeserved. We have been set free from the law and have received the Holy Spirit, who empowers us to be servants of God's new covenant. We have been set free from the need to veil our inadequacies, and can openly allow Jesus to work through us. We understand that we are fragile clay jars, designed to contain the treasure of the life of Jesus. Though the storms of life may threaten to crush us, we know that God will preserve us and never forsake us. Despite our temporary trials in this life, we can anticipate "the eternal weight of glory." We can seek to live to please Jesus until we see him face to face, exercising the ministry of reconciliation he has given us and fulfilling our calling as his ambassadors to a hurting world.

As you can see, living under the terms of the new covenant is radically different from living under the old covenant. I spent a decade living a "religious" life, thinking it was Christianity. I have often wondered if I would still be trapped in religion if I hadn't met Ray Stedman on that seminary retreat so many years ago. He not only taught those of us at the retreat the truth of the new covenant, he lived his life in the presence of God and the power of the Holy Spirit. He was truly free and spent his life showing others how to live in that same freedom. He summarized the new covenant in these important spiritual terms: "True Christianity is to manifest genuinely Christlike behavior by dependence on the working of the Spirit of God within, motivated by a love for the glory and honor of God."[19]

Now that you have spent some time examining these spiritual principles set forth by the Apostle Paul, let me ask you some crucial questions. Are you trying to live by the old covenant, yet sensing the futility of it? Or, can you say that you are in the process of understanding the new covenant, and enjoy trusting the Holy Spirit? My whole motivation for writing this book is that you would find true freedom, putting your whole trust in God, who can raise the dead.

Now is the Day of Salvation

Paul concludes this section with a quote from Isaiah the prophet. He explains that the door of salvation is now open for everyone because of the death and resurrection of God's son. Perhaps in reading this book, you have realized that Jesus has opened the door of salvation for you, too. He is inviting you to walk into his kingdom and receive the gift of eternal life. Remember his gracious words within his new covenant, as restated by David Roper: "God will be our God, and we will be his people. As we cast our lot with him and lay hold of his life, he will increasingly bestow on us his power for obedience and his forgiveness for weakness and failure." I encourage you to accept the Lord's invitation of salvation by simply placing your faith in Jesus as your Lord. He will then save you, forgive all your sins, and give you his Spirit to live out your new life for him. If you truly want to become one of his disciples, you can tell him in your own words or use the following words, realizing that God already knows what is in your heart.

Dear Jesus, I have sinned against you. I have not only sought to live out my life without you, but I have also refused to acknowledge you as my only Lord. I ask you by faith to become my Lord and forgive me of all my sins. Thank you for your forgiveness, the gift of eternal life, and the Holy Spirit. Thank you for the new covenant you are willing to make with me. I accept your gracious terms and will trust you to pro-vide the power to live within that covenant.

Now trust your new Lord Jesus to lead you in your new life with him. You will discover that you are finally *free at last* to love him and serve him the rest of your life on earth, and on into eternity.

NOTES

Chapter 1: **TO LOVE GOD**

1 John 8:31-32.

Chapter 2: **TO BE AT PEACE**

1 Ps. 29:11.
2 Charles Colson, *The Body: Being Light in Darkness* (Dallas: Word Publishing, 1992), 171.
3 See John 6:38, 12:49, John 14; Mark 1:35-39.
4 Luke 22:44-46.
5 John 17:13-21.
6 1 Pet. 2:20-23.
7 Acts 18:1-11.
8 2 Cor. 11:13.
9 1 Cor. 5:9-13.
10 2 Cor. 2:12-13.
11 Acts 16:9.
12 Rom. 10:9-13.
13 2 Cor. 7:5.
14 2 Cor. 2:14-17.
15 1 John 2:15-17.
16 2 Cor. 7:5-7.
17 1 Thess. 5:18.
18 Acts 27:35-36, emphasis mine.
19 Moses Hadas, *Imperial Rome* (New York: Time Incorporated, 1956), 57-68.
20 Rom. 8:1, 14-15.
21 See Exod. 24:3-8; Heb. 9:19-22.
22 See 2 Cor. 1:15-22.
23 2 Cor. 1:8-10, emphasis mine.
24 Acts 9:1-19.

Chapter 3: **TO BE COMPETENT**

1 Phil. 4:6.
2 2 Cor. 3:1-3.
3 2 Cor. 10:18.
4 1 Cor. 16.
5 1 Cor. 6:9-11.
6 Gal. 2:20.
7 Acts 18:9-10.
8 *National and International Religious Report*, 11 Jan. 1992.
9 John 16:7-11.
10 Titus 3:3-7.

11 John 1:12.
12 1 Cor. 6:19-20.
13 1 Cor. 12:12-13.
14 Eph. 1:13-14.
15 2 Cor. 3:4-6.
16 Phil. 3:1-16.
17 Phil. 4:13.
18 Luke 10:25-28.
19 2 Cor. 3:7, 9.
20 Rom. 7:7-12.
21 Ez. 16:60-63.
22 Is. 59:21.
23 Jer. 31:33-34
24 Heb. 13:20.
25 Luke 22:20.
26 David Roper, *The New Covenant In The Old Testament*, (Waco, Texas: Word Books, 1976, 25.
27 John 15:5.
28   2 Cor. 3:7-8.
29 Ex. 20:1-21.
30 2 Cor. 3:9-10.
31 2 Cor. 3:11.
32 Acts 1:2.
33 Ex. 4:10-12.

Chapter 4: **TO BE TRANSPARENT**

1 1 Cor. 8:3.
2 2 Cor. 3:12-13.
3 See 2 Cor. 1:8-11.
4 Jer. 31:31-34.
5 Luke 22:42.
6 2 Cor. 3:7.
7 Ex. 20-31.
8 See Ex. 32:19.
9 Ex. 34:29-35, emphasis mine.
10 2 Cor. 3:14-15.
11 See Ex. 24:3-8.
12 Deut. 5:29.
13 Phil. 3:4-6.
14 Ray C. Stedman, Discovery Paper no. 3681, Oct. 21, 1979.
15 Rom. 12:2.
16 2 Cor. 3:16-18.
17 See Ex. 34:34.
18 See Rom. 6:6-11.
19 Acts 4:7-13.

Chapter 5: **TO LIVE IN THE LIGHT**

1   John 3:21.
2   John 8:12.
3   Matt. 5:14-16.
4   *Common Ground*, Issue 78, Winter 93/94, 118.
5   2 Cor. 4:1-4.
6   Acts 16:21.
7   1 Cor. 6:12-13, 18-20.
8   2 Cor. 2:17.
9   Acts 15:1.
10 2 Cor. 6.
11 1 Thess. 4:3.
12 Rom. 1:18-21.
13 Mark 4:26-29.
14 2 Cor. 2:15-16.
15 2 Cor. 4:5-6.
16 Is. 53; Ps. 22.
17 Acts 2:22-32; 2 Sam. 7:22.
18 Acts 2:36.
19 Acts 22:4-8.
20 Acts 26:18.
21 Colson, The Body, 83.

Chapter 6: **TO DEAL WITH WEAKNESS**

1   Job 23:10.
2   2 Cor. 1:9.
3   2 Cor. 11:25-28.
4   2 Cor. 4:7-12.
5   Eugene Peterson, *The Message* (Colorado Springs: Navpress, 1993), 373.
6   Gal. 2:20.
7   Gen. 2:7.
8   Phil. 3:4-6.
9   Phil. 3:7-9.
10 Gen. 18:12-14.
11 Acts 7:25.
12 Ex. 3:6, 9-12.
13 Ex. 3:14.
14 Ex. 4:10.
15 Ex. 4:11-12.
16 Judges 6:4-6.
17 Judges 6:14.
18 Judges 6:16.
19 Judges 7:14.
20 2 Cor. 1:8-10.
21 Phil. 4:22.

22 J.I. Packer, *Knowing God* (Downers Grove, IL: InterVarsity Press, 1973), 227.

23 Acts 23:11.

24 Dietrich Bonhoeffer, *Letters and Papers from Prison* (New York: The Macmillan Company, 1953), 27.

25 Bonhoeffer, *Letters from Prison* , 14.

26 Acts 14.

27 2 Cor. 1:6.

28 1 Cor. 6:19-20.

29 2 Cor. 12:7-10.

30 Packer, Knowing God , 167.

31 2 Cor. 4:13-15.

32 Ps. 116:1-4.

33 Ps. 116:5-9.

34 Rev. 21:3-4.

35 Acts 18:9-11.

Chapter 7: **TO RESIST DISCOURAGEMENT**

1 1 Cor. 13:12.

2 1 Cor. 6:20.

3 2 Cor. 4:16.

4 2 Cor. 4:16-18.

5 Is. 40:28-31.

6 Luke 22:28-30.

7 Matt. 24:45-51.

8 Matt. 25:14-30.

9 John 15:16.

10 1 Cor. 3:1-8.

11 Heb. 12:2-3.

12 C. S. Lewis, *The Weight of Glory and Other Addresses*, (Grand Rapids: William B. Eerdmans Publishing Company, 1965), 7.

13 Eugene Peterson, The Message, 374.

14 2 Cor. 5:1-5.

15 William Barclay, *The Letters to the Corinthians* (Philadelphia: The Westminster Press, 1956), 228.

16 See 1 Cor. 15.

17 Matt. 17:1-3.

18 Luke 23:42-43, emphasis added.

19 See 1 Thess. 4:15-18; 1 Cor. 15:51-54.

20 Heb. 11:39-40. (For more insight into this concept, see Ray C. Stedman, *Authentic Christianity* (Portland: Multnomah Press), "Time and Eternity," 125-144.).

21 Eph. 1:13-14.

22 2 Cor. 5:6-10.

23 John 14:1-3.

24 Ps. 90:10,12.

25   John 5:19-20.
26   John 6:30.
27   John 12:49-50.
28   Acts 18:12.
29   See Matt. 25:31-46.
30   See Rev. 20:11-15.
31   1 Cor. 3:10-13.
32   1 Cor. 3:14-15.
33   Luke 21:1-4.
34   1 Cor. 4:3-5.
35   2 Tim. 4:6-8.

Chapter 8: **TO LIVE FOR JESUS**
1   1 Cor. 6:19.
2   2 Cor. 5: 11-13.
3   Deut. 10:12.
4   2 Cor. 5:14-15.
5   1 Tim. 1:15.
6   Rom. 5:12.
7   Eph. 2:1-3.
8   Rom. 5:8.
9   2Cor. 5:16-17
10   Matt. 21:9.
11   See Eph. 2:1-10.
12   2 Cor. 5:17.
13   1 Pet. 4:3-5, ff.
14   2 Cor. 5:18-19.
15   John 16:7-11.
16   Quoted in Charles Colson, *The Body*, 88.
17   2 Cor. 5:16-6:2.
18   1 Pet. 1:18-19.
19   Ray C. Stedman. "Legalism." Discovery Papers. May 14, 1972.